Code
s
nd
Edinburgh

20|20
VISIONS

20|20
VISIONS

COLLABORATIVE PLANNING AND PLACEMAKING

CHARLES CAMPION

RIBA Publishing

© RIBA Publishing, 2018

Published by RIBA Publishing, 66 Portland Place, London, W1B 1NT

ISBN 9781859467367/9781859467350 (PDF)

British Library Cataloguing-in-Publication Data
A catalogue record for this book is available from the British Library.

Commissioning Editor: Alexander White
Project Editors: Daniel Culver/Jane Rogers
Production: Jane Rogers
Designed and Typeset by Ashley Western
Printed and bound by Page Bros, Norwich
Cover design: Kneath Associates
Cover Image: Shutterstock.com

www.ribapublishing.com

CONTENTS

ACKNOWLEDGEMENTS

Writing this book has been a challenging but hugely enjoyable undertaking and my wife has been there all the way to discuss ideas and concepts and encourage me. Thank you, Lisa.

I would like to thank the following people for their inspiration, input and support. Thank you first to John Thompson, the founder Chairman of JTP, the energy and inspiration behind so many community planning Charrette processes that I have been privileged to be a part of. And to Harry "the Pencil" Harrison, whose special talent to interpret and illustrate placemaking concepts and Visions is displayed through a number of the case studies. I would like to thank managing partner Marcus Adams and all the partners at JTP for supporting the venture and encouraging me along the way.

Thank you to Debbie Radcliffe for sharing much of my community planning journey over the last 20 years and for her invaluable input into the book as a whole, and certain case studies in particular. Thank you to Bob Young for your insight and humour during many of the processes - I learnt a lot. Thank you to colleagues Adam Bowie, Dan Daley, Jenn Johnson and Leigh Yeats for their help researching, obtaining permissions and cataloguing the variety of images in the book.

Thank you to Robert Ivy from the American Institute of Architects for taking time to write such an elegant Foreword. Thank you to Angela Brady, past President of the RIBA for inviting me to contribute to her "British Papers" in 2015, which led to me submitting a proposal to RIBA Publishing for 20/20 Visions. Thank you to my colleagues at RIBA Publishing, in particular, my first Commissioning Editor Fay Gibbons and her successor Alexander White for their help and advice along the way.

Thank you to Joel Mills and Erin Simmons from the American Institute of Architects for their invaluable research and input into the history chapter, for introducing me to the communities and places of East Nashville and Santa Fe and for organising the Foreword from Robert Ivy. Thank you to Kobus Mentz and Susannah Goble from Urbanismplus. for supplying background material and input on Charrettes in Dunedin and Auckland. Thank you to Chip Kaufman and Wendy Morris from Ecologically Sustainable Design for their support and help with the Midland, Perth case study. Thank you to Professor Brian Evans and Graeme Pert who were so helpful with pulling together the Dumfries case study. Thank you to Fred London and Andreas von Zadow for their support and input to the Lübeck case study. Thank you to Chris Jones and Howard Bowcott for their support and input and for spending the day with me in Blaenau Ffestiniog

Thank you to many others who helped with the case study research in particular Suby Bowden and Gayla Bechtor for Santa Fe; Jonathan Davis, Roisin McDonough and Tony McCauley for Crumlin Road; Kieran Kinsella and Brian Hunt for Midland, Perth; Hunter Gee and Carol Pedigo for East Nashville; Nick Taylor and David Kelly for Scarborough; Halldora Hreggvisdottir and Ari Geirsson for Urridaholt; Marina Khoury and Xavier Iglesias and Matt Shillito for River District; Ben Bolgar, Ben Zucchi, Jim Chapman, David Houghton, Dr Jane Ratcliffe and Eleanor Brogan for Alder Hey; Ruth Cadbury MP, Judith Salomon and Malcolm Wood for Kew Bridge; Evelyn Hanlon and Ali Grehan for The Liberties; Veronica Eastell for Dunedin; Scott Dalgarno and David Cowie for Thurso and Wick; Kevin Collins, Richard Stay, Edward Irving and Alison Tero for Caddington; Steven Mindel and Emma Robinson from Barnes; Shujie Chen for Hangzhou; and Nicholas Boys Smith for Paddington Place.

Thank you to those who took time to meet with me and share their thoughts, experience and resources including, Andrés Duany, Bill Lennertz, Nick Wates, Paul Murrain, David Taylor, Nabeel Hamdi, Lynne Ceeney and Biljana Savic.

Like so many others, I am indebted to those who established the R/UDAT process in the United States 50 years ago and those who have spread the word and practice worldwide. And to clients from the public, private and community/third sectors who have commissioned Charrettes and given communities the opportunity to express their creativity.

TO LISA

FOREWORD

In a digitally frenetic time, when architectural technology has unleashed a plethora of unanticipated formal solutions to planning, design and construction, one humanely based architectural movement tied to democratic principles has thrived. Known by the acronym R/UDAT (Regional/Urban Design Assistance Team) this lauded programme has persisted for fifty years and spawned participatory charrette methodologies that flourish today – in North America and the UK, and around the world.

The relevance of democratic design is growing in this second decade of the twenty-first century. At a time in which societies all over the world are moving to cities at an unrelenting pace, and for the first time in human history, more of us live in cities than do not, the charrette model offers an optimistic perspective and an invaluable hands-on tool for city building.

The American Institute of Architects (AIA) is proud to have been associated with the development of charrettes through the R/UDAT programme, and we applaud the work illustrated in this book, which celebrates real results through case studies that demonstrate the diversity and richness of successful charrette methods, at a time when the world needs them more than ever.

Created in 1967 by AIA member Jules Gregory FAIA, and first held in Rapid City, South Dakota, the R/UDAT grew up and evolved in the civil rights era. Characteristic of their gestation in the 1960s, charrettes employ multidisciplinary teams of professionals to work with communities on a plan for urban change using the compressed timeframe. Today, after fifty years, over 150 R/UDATs have been organised by the AIA throughout North America, and the charrette methodology has been accepted and translated around the world.

Neither size nor scale limit the application of charrettes. Small towns and neighbourhoods, struggling economically, have seen light and hope, as have larger cities devastated by climatic events. In the US, universities, municipalities, state and federal agencies have adapted R/UDATs, and mayors have been among their most fervent admirers.

Millions of people today enjoy the results of charrette processes worldwide, and they have influenced professional practice as well. In the US, for example, the revitalisation of Portland's successful Pearl District came about through a R/UDAT, as did the Santa Fe Railyard redevelopment, and the renaissance of tornado-hit East Nashville, to name a few.

During the past fifty years, technological innovation has exploded. We all look to see how new tools will affect future planning. The more humble tools that spurred the earliest convocations, the ubiquitous pens and pads and tape, have been joined by architectural software and communication tools that enable visualisation, a way of seeing in three or four dimensions, or that allow collaboration to happen in easier, more seamless ways.

While the tools have changed, their fundamental purpose has not. The convening of citizens through charrettes – enlightened, purposeful and committed to design in its highest sense – offers hope for cities, towns and neighbourhoods struggling to find new models. Its democratic message explicitly promises us all that collective human intervention can be directed to positive ends.

ROBERT IVY FAIA
Executive Vice President and Chief Executive Officer
of the American Institute of Architects (AIA)

'To get rid of the habit of thinking of democracy as something institutional and external and to acquire the habit of treating it as a way of personal life is to realize that democracy is a moral ideal and so far as it becomes a fact is a moral fact. It is to realize that democracy is a reality only as it is indeed a commonplace of living.'

John Dewey
'Creative Democracy: The Task Before Us', 1939

PREFACE

I am always thoughtful when I walk through the doors of my local polling station to vote in a referendum or election. I think of my grandfather who fought in the First World War, and I think of my daughters and the world that they will inherit. I am fortunate to live in a mature, representative democracy, and consider it my duty to vote – but voting alone is not enough. We should in my view also expect to be involved in creatively shaping our futures in far more direct and participatory ways to achieve better, more sustainable outcomes – and we must be given the opportunity so to do.

I became interested in architecture and cities through my mother's encouragement to look around me and value my environment. My father taught me to respect and be respectful to others, whatever their background. Growing up in the 1960s and 1970s I noticed council housing tower blocks being erected that appeared ugly, with surrounding landscapes that quickly became degraded and threatening. Although people initially welcomed the new modern homes, these were not popular developments in the main, yet somehow they passed through the democratic planning system. Two or three decades later many of them were being demolished to make way for more traditional forms of housing.

I first became actively involved in my community when I noticed a new building in my town centre that jarred – I couldn't understand why the designers had chosen bricks that wilfully ignored the colour palette of the rest of the village. I joined the local residents' association to try to make a difference.

Then, in 1989, I started at Huddersfield School of Architecture. During my final year of the Architectural Studies (International) degree course we went on an epic field trip to India, and were given a site for our final degree project in a village near Delhi called Begumpur. I didn't know what urban design was at the time, but it seemed obvious to me that we should gain a greater understanding of the village context, and that included sitting down and talking with the local community.

When our group returned to the studio at Huddersfield, we intuitively drew up a series of analytical drawings. These were extremely important in our understanding of the community, the site and its context. Unfortunately, we discovered that there was no scope in the project mark scheme for credits to be attributed to what was an excellent piece of collaborative work. The three years degree was broad based and well delivered, but the thrust of architectural training it seemed was for students to solo-design object buildings with little reference to the community and context in which they would be sited.

On to Oxford Brookes University for two years' further study, and in the second year I signed up for the Urban Design Diploma. This was a gamechanger, a life changer. Lecture one was given by Ian Bentley, and from the first word it all made sense to me: urban design – transport, contextual buildings, streets and spaces, landscape and water, and COMMUNITY and ECONOMY. Tracing back from Jane Jacobs's *The Death and Life of Great American Cities* and on through to *Responsive Environments* by Bentley, Alcock, Murrain, McGlynn and Smith, efforts were clearly being made to rediscover the lost art of designing towns and cities around the needs and aspirations of local people and communities.

I began working in London with John Thompson & Partners (now JTP) in 1996 and was quickly immersed in collaborative placemaking through Community Planning Weekend (aka charrette) processes. One of the practice's core beliefs is that 'sustainable development is best achieved if the knowledge and commitment of local communities is engaged at every stage of the process'. Twenty-one years on and I have been involved in hundreds of participatory processes of various scales and types, both at home in the UK and internationally. I have seen again and again that involving people can break

ABOVE FIGURE 0.1:
South Acton Estate Community Planning Weekend, London, England, 1997

TOP FIGURE 0.2:
Shahama and Bahia charrette, Abu Dhabi, UAE, 2006

MIDDLE FIGURE 0.3:
Tanjung Ringgit EcoRegion™ workshops, Lombok, Indonesia, 2011

BOTTOM FIGURE 0.4:
Transport for Future Urban Growth Charrette, Auckland, New Zealand, 2016

down barriers, build community capacity, accelerate the decision-making process and lead to better, more sustainable places.

However, through my professional practice and in talking to numerous people when researching the case studies for this book, I have become aware that most people simply have no idea that there is a tried-and-tested methodology which could give them the opportunity to participate meaningfully in the planning of projects in their communities.

My aims in writing this book are threefold. First, I want people, politicians and professionals to know that there is an established methodology, the charrette, through which planning and placemaking professionals can work collaboratively with communities to bring mutual benefit. Second, I hope to inspire individuals and communities to demand the opportunity to participate in shaping plans and strategies for their areas to bring positive and lasting impacts to their own lives and those of future generations. And third, I hope that such participation becomes more commonly used to build consensus and create more innovative, sustainable and supported outcomes, tailored to each and every community, wherever they may be.

CHARLES CAMPION
RIBA AoU
2018
www.2020visionsbook.com

Sketch of a revitalised '100% corner'
from the East Nashville R/UDAT

CHAPTER|1
IT'S NOT ENOUGH TO VOTE

'The public is usually ahead of the political system.'
JOE BIDEN, FORMER US VICE PRESIDENT

The vote for Brexit in the UK in 2016, the rise of far-right leader Marine Le Pen in 2017 in France and the election of Donald Trump in 2016 in the US are signs of significant dissatisfaction with and disconnection from the political order in old, established democracies. This distrust of political institutions has arisen in parallel with a dissatisfaction with and disconnection from place-planning processes. All too often the planning system excludes meaningful input from communities, and is out of step with what these communities actually need and want. It is time to change the way things are done and to bring communities genuinely to the heart of planning and placemaking.

Cities, towns and villages were historically the product of many local hands, as places evolved to suit the economic, social and cultural needs of the community they served. However, the past few decades have seen planning theory and practice move away from creating locally distinctive and responsive places, in favour of delivering an agenda often imposed from outside the community. Planning has become dominated by professionals and politicians, and frequently it becomes adversarial as communities feel alienated, believing they have no real power to influence outcomes. The creativity of communities is a huge but largely untapped resource.

There is, however, a tried-and-tested collaborative planning methodology – the 'charrette' – which involves people in shaping the places in which they live. But charrettes are not universally known, and have even been described by some who have experienced them as 'the best kept secret'.

The charrette approach to planning involves members of the community working alongside local authorities and developers to co-create design-led, visual plans and strategies. It is an inspirational and energising activity where the results of collaboration are seen immediately, with the knowledge that each individual's input is listened to and actually matters. It also has the potential to speed up the formal design and planning process overall.

The word *charrette* is French for 'little cart'. In Paris in the nineteenth century, carts were sent around to collect the final drawings from students for display at *École des Beaux-Arts*. Students would jump on the carts to complete the presentations right up to the deadline. Today the word has been taken to describe an intensive, collaborative planning process in which designers, the community and others work together to create a vision for a place or development. The concept of placemaking is used as a lens through which to assess issues and propose actions – not just for physical plans, but for social and economic solutions too.

This book explores and promotes the benefits of participatory and democratic planning and placemaking through charrettes. Its timing was inspired by the fiftieth anniversary in 2017 of the first American Institute of Architects (AIA) Regional/Urban Design Assistance Team (R/UDAT). In 1967, in response to a request from the business community in Rapid City, South Dakota, the AIA dispatched a group of architects and planners to work with the local community over a weekend to produce a revitalisation strategy in an early charrette process. Over the last fifty years charrettes have gone on to make a global impact by involving people in a form of participatory democracy – not relying on elected representatives to make decisions on their behalf, but having a direct creative input into and influence on the decisions themselves.

As well as the use of words and numbers, often the sole tools of public debate and decision making, charrettes add the medium of drawing, so vital when discussing and formulating proposals for 'place'. People are empowered to get on with designing and delivering solutions that are right for their own particular area. Charrettes encourage joined-up thinking and holistic visioning, which in turn can lead to appropriate short-, medium- and long-term actions.

From a professional perspective, charrettes provide an efficient working process that enables design teams to set up their studio in the location of the charrette and focus solely on the project at hand, covering a great deal of ground over a few days. Contact with the community brings local knowledge and creativity into the process, and helps develop plans and solutions that have wide support.

One of the key characteristics of charrettes is flexibility. The case studies in Chapter 5 illustrate the variety of scenarios a charrette can serve, from co-designing flood-protection measures, to masterplanning previously developed, historically sensitive sites, and creating the early vision for a Local Development Plan.

The book begins with a historical overview of the development and use of charrette methodologies, which began in the US and then spread internationally.

The next chapter is an exploration of why charrettes are important, how they achieve holistic outcomes through intensive multiday processes facilitated by a multidisciplinary team, and suggested ways forward for promoting collaborative planning processes.

Charrette processes are given different names and have subtly different methodologies, depending on the practitioners involved and the countries in which they take place. Chapter 3 describes a charrette methodology in order to make clear its fundamental simplicity, but also the need for careful and inclusive organisation. There is information about pre-charrette preparation, and a generic example of a charrette illustrated with images from a real-life charrette. The chapter concludes with a selection of post-charrette follow-on scenarios, all-important in maintaining momentum and continuing community involvement in actually delivering and managing the project. A question John Thompson, a pioneer of Community Planning in the UK, frequently poses is: 'Who decides, who delivers and who maintains?'

The core of the book focuses on twenty diverse international case studies, which include UK and international examples of charrettes, with some involving JTP and others led by practices from around the world. The case studies explain the historical, social and cultural milieu of the places, the charrette process and the outcomes, with comments from participants interspersed throughout. There is discussion of key themes, and a description of the consensual visions that have resulted from each process.

The book ends with an overview of the key lessons learned from the case studies.

I have had the privilege of meeting and speaking with many people while researching this book. In writing the case studies I have only been able to mention a small number of those involved. People I approached have been unfailingly generous with their time, and in offering useful material. I would like to thank everyone.

The case studies show that charrettes in all their guises have been used as a valuable tool in a wide range of circumstances. The process has inspired and involved large numbers of people in many different countries; it has true global appeal. This book, and the stories within it, should provide a stimulus for collaborative placemaking events, which I believe should be promoted to have the widest possible use, in the greatest number of places.

CHAPTER | 2

A HISTORY OF COLLABORATIVE PLANNING AND THE CHARRETTE PROCESS

> 'Cities are political ecologies.'
> PETER CALTHORPE, CALTHORPE ASSOCIATES

The success of humankind on Earth is to a large degree a function of our ability to socialise and to collaborate in performing tasks such as hunting and building shelter. The African proverb 'It takes a village to raise a child' recognises the necessity of multiple inputs and collaboration in nurturing and raising children for the mutual benefit of all members of the community.

When telling the story of collaborative charrette processes, historians often refer back to the Amish tradition of barn raising – events in which community members cooperate to build a barn, or other structure, in a day. Typically, the eventual owner of the barn undertakes the advanced organisation, including site preparation and ordering of materials, to ensure the best and most effective outcomes from the cooperative barn-raising day.

Nineteenth-century thinkers contemplated ideal human environments in response to the industrialisation of the time, and its impact on population growth and creating cramped and unhealthy living conditions in cities. William Morris, Patrick Geddes and Ebenezer Howard were all hugely influential in planning theory, and proposed models for balanced, communitarian living in harmony with nature and to facilitate food growing. Buildings, neighbourhoods and cities were viewed as being the product of many skills and many hands. It was seen that urban environments should be laid out to promote healthy living, rewarding work and access to green space and the countryside for food and leisure. Governance was a crucial factor in realising and sustaining such visions, with a key element being the active involvement of citizens in their neighbourhood communities.

The origin of the modern, multiday charrette process has been credited to the Caudill Rowlett Scott (CRS) 'Squatters'. In 1948 CRS, an architectural practice based in Austin, Texas, was working on a school project in Blackwell, Oklahoma. To avoid time-consuming and energy-sapping travel, the team established a temporary office on site and worked collaboratively with the school board over a few days to resolve the design. Bill Caudill of CRS was interviewed in 1971. He recalled that by the end of the week, they had unanimous and enthusiastic board approval for the project: 'While we were trying to solve a communication problem we discovered something that we should have known all along – to involve the users in the planning process.'[1] This novel way of working proved so effective that CRS incorporated multiday Squatters into future projects as a way of involving clients, users and a multidisciplinary team to build consensus and support.

The 1960s was a seminal decade in American history, and marked a wave of civic engagement and service. In 1961 John F. Kennedy's famous inauguration speech challenged Americans to renew their spirit of public service, famously stating: 'Ask not what your country can do for you, but what you can do for your country.'[2] Nothing was more influential on the emergence of mainstream collaborative planning than the collective impact of the civil rights movement. The groundswell of urban voices calling for equality and involvement in the decision-making processes surrounding cities was impossible to ignore. Experimentation with new ideas and practices grew and evolved in response to the tumultuous events of the era, and these included a key part of the charrette story, the R/UDAT.

At the time, the critique of the status quo and conventional thinking about cities was gaining momentum. Much of the criticism focused on the policies of the US urban renewal programme, which had a devastating impact on many urban communities. The construction of interstate highways increased white migration to the suburbs, while simultaneously creating physical barriers within cities. Highway projects frequently led to the demolition of inner-city neighbourhoods and the displacement of poor residents, and were used as a form of slum clearance. By the 1960s the impact of these policies was becoming clear, and between 1949 and 1973 more than 2,000 projects in cities had resulted in the demolition of over 600,000 homes and the displacement of over two million people.[3]

Jane Jacobs's landmark work, *The Death and Life of Great American Cities*, published in 1961, was highly critical of 'orthodox' city planning. The book articulated a series of principles for producing vibrant places, and it expressed and demonstrated the value of the 'citizen expert'. She famously declared: 'Cities have the capability of providing something for everybody, only because, and only when, they are created by everybody.'[4]

The design and planning professions responded to these challenges by pioneering new approaches. In 1963, David Lewis and Ray Gindroz co-founded Urban Design Associates (UDA), a firm with high ideals. As Lewis described: 'At UDA, we learned a basic lesson from the groundswell of courage that lay at the heart of the civil rights movement and its dedication to the principles of democracy. Our accountability as urban designers has always been to the voices of citizens and to their vision for the future of their communities.'[5] This democratic concept of design was revolutionary in the 1960s, as it elevated citizens to a co-designing relationship with professionals, and empowered them in the creation of their communities.

In addition to the enduring inequalities of the 1960s, the lack of any form of consultation or involvement with the residents who were directly affected by slum clearance and highway projects led to a boiling point of civic frustration, culminating in a wave of unrest. In 1967, the US experienced what is commonly referred to as the 'long hot summer', a series of over 150 riots in cities across the country, as anger at inequality boiled over. That year also saw the birth of the R/UDAT.

The individual credited with the idea for the first R/UDAT was the architect Jules Gregory, then Vice President of the AIA. David Lewis described him as: 'The great hero of modern American architecture. He stepped out and tried to lead a new idea, which was the idea of architects in service to society.'

The first R/UDAT project took place in June 1967, in response to a visit to the AIA by James Bell, the President of the Chamber of Commerce in Rapid City, South Dakota. The downtown area had suffered from serious flooding, and had also been in decline for years. James Bell was looking for help to produce a revitalisation strategy. After intense discussions about the reasons for the decline, the AIA agreed to send a team of four – two architects and two planners – to Rapid City to give assistance.

The team met key stakeholders such as the mayor and the city council, as well as local architects, the media and selected citizens. Meetings were informal, with the intention being to hear all sides of the various issues that were raised. The team then reviewed written information about Rapid City in the light of what they heard from their engagement with members of the community. They gave a verbal presentation of their findings, and a week or so later provided Rapid City with a brief written report and recommendations.

The process triggered unexpected changes. A planning commission was established, which included one of the local architects. The city hired a full-time planner and engaged a consultant to help. A wide variety of individuals, government officials, businesspeople and ordinary citizens were made aware of important local issues, and learned to debate them together. Everyone who was involved – including the visiting team – came to see that 'in a few short and crowded days the community, with a modicum of stimulus and help from the outside, had resources within it that it could learn to harness in the public interest'.[6]

The R/UDAT team was struck by where the experience led them. It turned out that the most significant achievement of the Rapid City R/UDAT was not physical at all – at least not to begin with. It was the impact on public policy that made the greatest waves, through a process of democratic exchange. The value of the process was clear to the AIA Urban Planning and Design Committee, which decided to offer the idea to other communities – and so R/UDAT was born.

In 1969, enough early work and experimentation in participatory planning had occurred to enable development of a theory of public participation.

Sherry Arnstein published 'A Ladder of Citizen Participation' in the *Journal of the American Institute of Planners*,[7] articulating a framework within which to consider contemporary approaches to engaging citizens in public work. The different levels of involvement on each rung, from Manipulation and Therapy on the bottom two rungs, to Delegated Power and Citizen Control at the top, made it possible to understand the increasing demands for participation from the have-nots, as well as the gamut of confusing responses from the holders of power. This framework would become a seminal work in understanding early mistakes in and the evolution of collaborative planning.

As its most important philosophical principle, R/UDAT elevated the citizen as co-designer through its emphasis on broad participation and a community-driven process.

By 1971, charrettes were being openly promoted as a successful tool through the *AIA Journal*. The AIA's support for such practices also marked a significant development for the field of urban design. Ray Gindroz from UDA noted: 'R/UDATs as an official AIA function meant that urban design was something that architects were actively engaged in. It gave tremendous visibility for the profession of urban design and it helped

establish its credibility.'[8] At the same time, participatory models began to be used in the international aid and development sector, which had become over-complex and was often not dealing with problems in a way that reflected local conditions.

Architect Nabeel Hamdi recognised that people receiving international aid were being treated as beneficiaries of charity; many aid programmes were wasteful and lacked dignity and social intelligence.[9]

Collaborative planning methodologies began to be employed to co-design and co-deliver appropriate solutions both in the built environment and in social provision and self-governance. As a consequence, development programmes became more focused on local problems and directed at local opportunities to deliver achievable actions.

In the 1980s, the R/UDAT process gained considerable traction with internationally adapted models. Events in the US were noticed in Canada, and the Committee for an Urban Study Effort (CAUSE) was established and went on to organise and conduct projects in over thirty communities during the following decade.

Charrettes were becoming known as a quick and efficient design team-working process. Developer Robert Davis suggested a charrette methodology when developing the proposals for Seaside, Florida with Andrés Duany, Elizabeth Plater-Zyberk (founders of DPZ) and Léon Krier because, in his words, 'I didn't want to spend a year developing a masterplan'. Speed and efficiency, two of the key benefits of charrette processes, were being increasingly appreciated by the development sector.

Meanwhile in the UK, following significant unrest in post-industrial cities in the early 1980s, a new community architecture movement emerged, which embraced community planning, community design, community development and community technical aid. It came from a growing realisation that, despite the best intentions of postwar planning, the poor design and mismanagement of the built environment was a major contributor to the nation's social and economic ills.

This interest in co-design led to transatlantic conversations between the AIA and the Royal Institute of British Architects (RIBA), and the formation of the Community Urban Design Assistance Team (C/UDAT) programme. Although the C/UDAT programme was short-lived, the community architecture movement continued to gain momentum. In 1986, the movement held a seminal event, Building Communities, the First International Conference on Community Architecture, which was attended by more than 1,000 participants.

The ongoing transatlantic collaboration culminated in the Remaking Cities Conference in Pittsburgh, Pennsylvania in 1988, which brought together 400 experts and citizens from both sides of the Atlantic. The event was jointly sponsored by the AIA and the RIBA, with HRH The Prince of Wales chairing the conference and delivering the keynote address. David Lewis served as co-chair, and in his opening remarks he left no doubt as to the focus of the event: 'This will be a conference about democracy, a conference about how to make democracy work, how to improve our cities, how to improve our standards of life.'[10]

The event marked a historic moment not only in thinking about post-industrial cities, but also regarding the evolution of collaborative planning. Rod Hackney, then President of the RIBA, suggested a new way of doing business in the UK: 'A partnership of enterprise is what I'm calling for, a partnership between builders, professionals and politicians – local, state and national. And most important of all, with ordinary people – the people who count, local people, who at the moment aren't seen as part of any formula for success. But we must make sure they are.'

As a part of the conference, an R/UDAT was organised to focus on the lower Monongahela Valley in Pennsylvania to open up the subject of how post-industrial communities might best face their challenges. A bi-national team was formed to collaborate on the project, featuring eighteen professionals from the US and the UK. For the first time UK-based architects saw in action this methodology for working with communities to create plans and visions for their area.

On returning from Pittsburgh, practitioners began organising charrette processes in the UK. In 1989, John Thompson facilitated the UK's first charrette, the Vision for Bishopsgate Goods Yard Community Planning Weekend.

Other practitioners also developed collaborative planning processes, such as the Prince's Foundation's Enquiry by Design charrette methodology, and programmed their events using combinations of activities that they felt worked best for them, such as urban design community training sessions, open-space dialogue workshops, site walkabouts, facilitated design tables and plenary report back sessions.

Charrettes have come to be accepted for use at a range of project scales, in both the public and private sectors. The effectiveness of the process has also influenced professional practice, with design teams adopting charrette-style approaches for internal team working.

Working with communities is a natural and central part of the philosophy of New Urbanism, and charrettes have been adopted as a key tool by leading New Urbanist practitioners.

DPZ developed its own brand of charrette process and inspired a generation of practitioners, who spread out around the world. Chip Kaufman, who organised charrettes for DPZ in the late 1980s and early 1990s, describes the spread: 'It was like spontaneous combustion; the need was there.' Chip and his partner Wendy Morris went on to deliver scores of charrette processes around Australia and internationally from their base in Melbourne. Another former DPZ employee, Bill Lennertz, co-founded the National Charrette Institute in Portland, Oregon, dedicated to training and supporting professionals and communities.

In 1993, many US built environment professionals, concerned with prevailing anti-urban development patterns, in particular urban sprawl, formed the influential Congress for New Urbanism (CNU). The CNU advocates walkable, neighbourhood-based development and a commitment to 're-establishing the relationship between the art of building and the making of community, through citizen-based participatory planning and design'.[11]

Charrette processes have focused not just on design outcomes but also on establishing governance mechanisms, such as Town Teams and Community Trusts. Alan Simpson, also a participant at the Remaking Cities Conference in 1988, went on to head up the Yorkshire Forward Urban Renaissance Programme, which was initiated in 2001. As well as working with communities to co-design placemaking visions for their towns and cities, the programme set up Town Teams, through which citizens were empowered to sign off public funds coming into their town.

Over the past fifty years, an entirely new orientation to public work in our cities has emerged. The context and realities of urban work today are in many ways wholly different from how it was. Jane Jacobs's *The Death and Life of Great American Cities* is now the de facto urban planning bible. It has sold over 250,000 copies and has been translated into six languages. During the past half-century, R/UDATs and related collaborative planning practices have influenced millions of people internationally and helped contribute to how we think about cities, towns and villages today.

In England, the localism agenda has substantiated that the public can have statutory control, and encouraged communities to co-design Neighbourhood Plans to determine and promote development in their areas. Civic Voice, the national charity for civic societies, has promoted charrette methodologies through its publication 'Collaborative Planning for All'.

In Scotland, the government has been promoting and funding charrette processes nationally since 2011, as part of the Sustainable Communities Initiative. Around the UK, promoters of large-scale developments are encouraged to undertake visioning processes with communities, including design workshops, to help shape proposals prior to the submission of planning applications.

However, collaborative planning is still not universally recognised as the most effective way to approach placemaking strategies. It remains an alternative to mainstream, conventional community consultation that is much more cursory in nature.

In recent years, there has been an attack on the use of collaborative planning that is largely motivated by poor experiences, which have resulted in controversy and conflict. Nimbyism (not in my back yard) has grown as a phenomenon, and many communities have developed well-organised campaigns against development proposals, making collaborative processes sometimes difficult to negotiate. As a result, some professionals have begun to advocate for a return to professionally driven placemaking, decrying the public opposition to their ideas as a stumbling block to achieving more sustainable communities.

Advocating the old 'top down' ways is a dangerous path, however, which will inevitably lead to more disconnect between built environment professionals and communities.

Others say that collaborative planning may no longer be necessary because of technological applications which gather user data so easily, and that this can define public opinion at a much larger scale than most participatory processes. However, much of the data accumulated is about an individual's use of the urban environment, and cannot serve visioning or collaborative planning purposes. Not all matters can be reduced to a binary yes/no response. Creating plans requires an iterative process of collaborative discussion, clarification and learning, which a click on an internet survey will never manage to capture. In practice, it will downgrade citizens to mere consumers.

'Although there are increasingly sophisticated online engagement tools, nothing can replace face-to-face communication and joint decision making through structured, collaborative design processes, where concerns and ideas are shared ... enabling local people to have a greater understanding and sense of ownership of the resulting policies and proposals.'

Biljana Savic
Churchill Fellowship Research, 2014

While collaborative planning is not always an easy or comfortable route to successful development, it exposes professionals to the rigours of debate and questioning, which is crucial for professional development and democratic process.

As the case studies in this book demonstrate, most charrette processes are run in an appreciative and positive environment. They should be properly resourced and carefully programmed, with a clear mission statement about aims and expectations and an acceptance of the value of robust debate. Clarity on how the process will continue after the charrette is also important.

Collaborative planning processes have as much or more currency and relevance today as they did fifty years ago. As David Lewis, the founder of much of the philosophy and experiments of the 1960s collaborative planning efforts maintains: 'Perhaps the most important gift of those decades was to return to us our passion for democracy – a gift that today we need to refurbish once again.'[12]

CHAPTER | 3

THE IMPORTANCE OF COLLABORATION

'There are a lot of us and we all live together and we all need to be recognised and satisfied and heard.'

IGGY POP

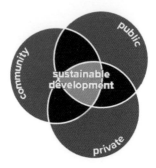

FIGURE 3.1:

Sustainable development occurs when people are part of the planning and placemaking process

Human beings are naturally collaborative and proactive in creating their own habitats. Most of the world's population now live in urban environments, and the majority of people want to live in the enterprising and sustainable communities that traditional planning seeks to support and deliver. But professionals and politicians tend to dominate planning and placemaking, which means that communities can become alienated from the process.

Communities are all too often only 'consulted' on proposals that have already been formulated without their input, and see themselves as being excluded from the real decision making, which usually takes place before the 'consultation' stage even begins. This can lead to poor decisions that ignore local knowledge and needs. Proposals that are not supported by the wider community often lead to opposition campaigns and costly delays in the planning process.

Nicholas Boys Smith, from the London-based urban thinktank Create Streets, highlights research[13] that shows a cavernous divide between the professional and the layperson on what is viewed as good and bad architecture. For this reason, he promotes the idea that urban planning and development must acknowledge what people want, because if it is left up to the professional, citizens will continue to live with ill-advised buildings and streetscapes that do not suit their needs and desires.

David Halpern's 1995 publication, *Mental Health and the Built Environment*, describes architecture and planning as subjective and lacking the empirical tradition that would make it legible to the scientific eye.[14] His book considers several issues that arise when trying to identify and analyse the built environment's impact on stress, personal relationships and the relationships between the environment's symbolic elements. From his analyses, it is clear that people experience the built environment in vastly different ways, and that this paradox should be central to placemaking.

Drawing on the disciplines of psychology, neuroscience and urban planning, Charles Montgomery in *Happy City* describes how cities affect how we think, feel and behave.[15] He argues that the green city, the low-carbon city and the happy city are the same thing, and happiness is not just the pleasure of it; it is through being an active member of society that we become happier.

Research published by the Prince's Foundation in 2014 concluded that: 'People want where they live to be more than just a building. They want it to be somewhere distinct, somewhere that enhances their quality of life: a place. Creating places goes beyond merely creating spaces – it means designing buildings that cater to the needs of residents, supporting quality public spaces and providing opportunities for communities to thrive.' It continues: 'Perhaps above all, communities want to be genuinely involved in a real, not stage-managed, consultation process.'[16]

'Use development as an opportunity to engage with the community and explore the opportunities.'

David Partridge,
Managing Partner,
Argent LLP, developer of King's Cross London

The quality and functioning of a city, town or village is critical to the realisation of shared objectives across the political spectrum: local prosperity, economic growth, and access to jobs and training, culture and heritage, social integration and equity, community safety and health and wellbeing. Communities want to have a say, and many want the opportunity to participate in shaping the design and governance of their place so that it reaches its full potential for the people who live and work there.

Full participation, in a properly organised collaborative charrette process, is about incorporating the community's knowledge into the process, and working with professionals to create better proposals, and therefore better places. Improving the quality of life becomes a shared goal around which a vision of the future and specific projects can then be developed. It provides a way for individuals within the community to offer local expertise, creativity and enthusiasm, and to work with professionals and strangers as well as friends, family and neighbours. Actively engaging communities early in the planning process can result in substantial benefits to economic, environmental and social sustainability.

Charrettes have a key role to play, and the experience and knowledge base built up by practitioners over the past fifty years should be expanded on to develop skills, resources, policies and funding to move charrettes into the mainstream.

Professional and community organisations should:

• Run publicity campaigns to promote the benefits of charrette processes to politicians, local authorities, developers and communities

• Establish programmes of funded charrette pilot projects for communities, to explore how early and meaningful participation can result in a positive approach to growth, development and change

• Strengthen planning policy to require collaborative, charrette-based planning for major developments and in preparing Local Plans

• Adapt planning policy to recognise when charrettes have been undertaken so that future stages in the process fully take account of those community decisions, and provide ongoing support for them

• Promote the use of design codes with community input as part of the planning process to ensure outputs from collaborative planning and placemaking processes are delivered

• Promote open planning negotiations regarding community benefits from developments, so that when charrettes are held a proportion of the community benefit funding is allocated to the community involved, e.g. Community Trusts, subsidised workspaces, movement and transport infrastructure

• Make improving the quality of the public realm in cities, towns and villages a priority, and require every local authority to produce a Place Improvement Strategy and Place Charter

• Promote and fund Town Teams with administrative support to involve businesses, creative economy and community groups to review visions and management strategies, and sign off placemaking funding for projects

• Train built environment students in collaborative working methods including charrette systems

• Promote and encourage awareness of design and urbanism among all school-age students, and enable their participation in charrettes

• Set up civic design centres or 'urban rooms', where communities can go to understand and debate the past, present and future of their place with a physical or virtual model

A combination of these initiatives will help to bring collaborative processes into mainstream planning and placemaking. Through shared working from an early stage, communities and businesses can help shape and support development that is right for their specific place, and will enable it to grow and thrive.

CHAPTER | 4
WHAT IS COLLABORATIVE PLANNING AND PLACEMAKING?

'The essence of community planning is simple – all around us we are surrounded by people who have within themselves, whether they recognise it or not, a great wealth of common intelligence and knowledge. If we can tap that knowledge and intelligence we can enrich all the processes that we are involved in, we can bring about much better solutions and we can even involve the people in sustaining these solutions in the future.'

JOHN THOMPSON, FOUNDER CHAIRMAN, JTP,
AND HONORARY PRESIDENT, ACADEMY OF URBANISM (AOU)

When considering the future of a place there are numerous ways of connecting communities and gathering information, including surveys, questionnaires, social media, one-to-one interviews, world cafe events, citizens' juries and focus groups. These can be valuable at various stages of a participation process, but it is the face-to-face coming together of the community in a structured and facilitated charrette, with open dialogue and co-design, that has been found to be most effective in enabling communities to address change, build consensus and create a holistic vision for their place.

Charrettes are multiday collaborative events that connect local people with expert facilitation in co-creating spatial designs and action plans. They form a hands-on approach with stated goals that allows for iterative feedback and design changes, which is important for gaining stakeholder understanding and support.

A neutral team of facilitators and relevant advisors treats everyone present as having an equal right to take part in the process. Physical, social, commercial and environmental issues are addressed holistically through a combination of dialogue workshops (often using sticky notes) and hands-on co-design sessions. The views of all members of the community – including young people – are sought, and everyone is given a chance to exercise their creativity.

A key reason why charrettes are shown to be so effective is that the time and space programmed into the process allows for the incorporation of 'feedback loops', so that ideas can be presented, discussed and tested, worked on further, re-presented and so on.

'The Zen of Charrettes'[17] describes how it can take multiple interactions with a person or group to transform from a position of resistance to a position of listening and then to a position of understanding. 'Openness and listening replaces ego. Participants develop trust in this authentically open design process that seeks the best solution, regardless of its source. Shared learning takes place during each feedback session among specialists and community members.'

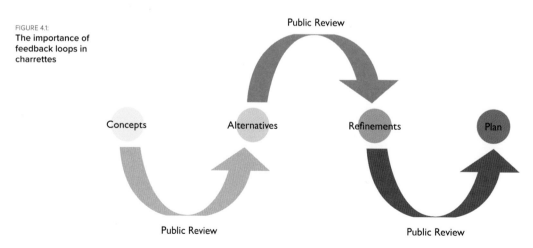

FIGURE 4.1:
The importance of feedback loops in charrettes

Public Review

Concepts   Alternatives   Refinements   Plan

Public Review   Public Review

Community participation, through early, inclusive, collaborative methods, should be supported and embedded at all tiers of planning to generate a common sense of ownership and to deliver high-quality, enterprising and sustainable places.

BENEFITS OF CHARRETTES:

- They bring communities, local authorities and development professionals together to focus on positive solutions
- They bring together a multidisciplinary team to focus on one project
- They bring local knowledge into the process
- They resolve complex, multilayered problems
- They speed up the planning process
- They break down barriers within a community and foster community cohesion
- They raise levels of aspiration and build capacity within a community
- They increase environmental awareness and the social and economic value of place
- They enable identification of new community champions
- They create shared visions, a positive approach to change and better outcomes

STARTING THE CHARRETTE
INVOLVING IMPLEMENTERS

For charrettes to be most effective they should, when possible, involve the policymakers and the teams who will lead the implementation. Success is most likely when charrettes are used to establish a dialogue between the community and the developers and/or planning policymakers who are committed to proceeding with the funding and implementation of a project. This enables the community's knowledge about their place to be brought into the debate through iterative design and discussions. This being said, charrettes have been employed to broaden the understanding of an issue and widen the debate about the future of a place without the key protagonists being involved – in these cases the participants should be made aware of the basis on which they are participating, and that the charrette organisers have no direct control over implementation.

CHARRETTES CAN BE USED FOR:

- Local Plans
- Regional and sub-regional strategies and plans
- Planning garden cities, villages and neighbourhoods
- Neighbourhood Plans
- Visioning for Regeneration Plans
- Planning of large developments and strategic housing allocations
- Planning landscape and transport strategies
- Designing new neighbourhoods and urban regeneration, including architectural design

When organising a charrette, the seven core values drawn up by the International Association for Public Participation are useful to consider and agree on:[18]

• Public participation is based on the belief that those who are affected by a decision have a right to be involved in the decision-making process

• Public participation includes the promise that the public's contribution will influence the decision

• Public participation promotes sustainable decisions by recognising and communicating the needs and interests of all participants, including decision-makers

• Public participation seeks out and facilitates the involvement of those potentially affected by or interested in a decision

• Public participation seeks input from participants in designing how they participate

• Public participation provides participants with the information they need to participate in a meaningful way

• Public participation communicates to participants how their input affected the decision

FUNDING
A key determinant of the shape of the process will be the funding mechanisms. Developer-led charrettes are likely to be resourced as part of the planning process for a particular site, and are therefore also likely to be well funded. In some cases, site owners, such as public sector agencies working in partnership with a chosen developer, may require a collaborative process to make sure solutions, once implemented, will bring benefits to the wider community. Public or third-sector charrettes looking to create a planning framework for a site or a wider planning policy document may be funded by central or local government, or attract grants and funding from bodies such as a Lottery fund, or through philanthropy, social investment funds, crowdfunding, partnering with private developers and so on. In some cases, part of the condition for the funding may be the involvement of the community in the planning process.

Where charrettes are promoted and organised by the community or voluntary sector themselves, similar funding sources should be investigated. In addition, communities and voluntary sector bodies may secure resources in the form of donations and pro bono professional work. Other innovations by this sector can also deliver significant outcomes for little financial outlay. Examples include holding open design competitions with community engagement specified in the brief, or developing campaigns promoting certain policies or strategies that will attract interest from professionals willing to commit resources to the cause.

EARLY INVOLVEMENT
Communities should be involved from an early stage in the creation of Area Regeneration Plans, Local Development Plans, Area Action Plans, Town Centre Regeneration Strategies, and when planning urban extensions and other significant sites. Charrette processes should be appropriately planned according to the project and process – and as a result, charrette programmes may vary.

PREPARATION
Once resources are in place and it has been decided to organise a charrette, it is important to prepare the process carefully.

STEERING GROUP
The collaborative planning process will typically be started several months before the charrette event by setting up a steering group to meet regularly and

plan the event. The steering group should be made up of the process promoters, such as the planning policy or development team, and a wide range of local stakeholders, including local community and amenity organisations, businesses, landowners and local authorities. New members may join over time.

The first task of the steering group is to agree a mission statement – i.e. what the aims of the process are. Other key tasks include agreeing a date and venue for the charrette, and any pre-event activities, including the launch. The charrette programme will need to be designed, together with the timing and nature of the reporting back.

COMMUNICATION STRATEGY

A suitable date for the charrette should be chosen that does not clash with important local or national holidays and events. Decisions should be taken as to whether a website should be set up for the process, or whether existing websites or social media should be used. Whatever platform is chosen, it should be well maintained and monitored, and should promote information about the forthcoming charrette, including relevant background and contact information. There should ideally be a mechanism to post published information, including technical reports and feedback presentations and documents. This could include an online form for people to make comments. If a website is set up or used, social media can also play its part in publicising the charrette and gathering feedback – live social media feeds such as Twitter or Facebook can be interesting additions to events, increasing the interactivity of the process.

It will be necessary to develop a database of all contacts for communication by letter, email or phone as the process progresses, while ensuring that local data protection legislation is adhered to. Contacts can include national political representatives, local council members and officers, schools and educational institutions, police,

utility providers and agencies, faith groups, youth groups, Scout and Guide groups, amenity groups, arts and local history groups, sports and leisure organisations, business groups, civic societies, residents' associations and any others who might have an interest in the future of their place.

STAKEHOLDER HIERARCHY

Charrettes are broadly democratic in that they bring the voice of citizens directly into the planning and design process. However, it is important to understand the need to first make direct contact with elected and group representatives, local authority departments and those with a special place in the process, such as landowners and those directly affected by the proposals. Having discussed the project with the local authority officers, local politicians, as elected representatives, should be contacted initially to ensure they are briefed about the process and can provide useful information about the community and local issues and aspirations. Local landowners, residents and businesses directly impacted by what may happen should also receive focused attention, followed by local groups and organisations. The wider community will be then contacted via broader-based publicity and encouraged to participate in the charrette process.

> **NOTE:** There are occasions where stakeholder only events are held, either as a first step to an open event, or because it is felt that this is sufficient for gaining the level of input required for a particular process.

PRE-EVENT LAUNCH

It is a good idea to launch the process to an audience of invited stakeholders, to gain media attention and ensure that accurate information is disseminated at an early stage of the process. The launch also provides an opportunity to explain the upcoming charrette process to invitees. It may also be appropriate to hold a scoping workshop with those present at the launch to begin the process of understanding local issues and aspirations, and to start designing the charrette process. Key stakeholders will be able to meet members of the charrette facilitation team and start to build relationships. Stakeholders can then act as ambassadors for the process to the wider community.

PUBLICITY

Following the launch, every effort should be made to promote the charrette, through flyers including details of the event programme, articles and advertisements in the local media, posters on local authority noticeboards and in shop windows, banners at suitable locations,

and through social media. If the charrette is related to a specific development site it is important to ensure that households and businesses in nearby streets receive hand-delivered flyers. The publicity strategy must aim to ensure that the community is fully aware of the upcoming charrette.

SURVEYS

Organising a community survey in the run-up to the charrette is a good way of collating baseline information about community views, while publicising the event at the same time.

ANIMATING THE COMMUNITY

Community animation in the weeks preceding the charrette is important to ensure that local groups and key stakeholders, including schools, youth clubs and neighbourhood groups, are prepared for the event and to explain why everyone's participation at the charrette is important. Useful information and further contacts can be gleaned from conversations at places where people

FIGURE 4.2:
St Clement's Community Planning Workshops and Exhibition Charrette in London was launched close to the site to invited stakeholders and the local media

naturally gather, for example shops, community centres, bus stops, pubs and recreation grounds, and by attending local fetes and carnivals. This is a way to acquire local knowledge, gain trust, provide information and generate enthusiasm for the collaborative planning process.

INVOLVING YOUNG PEOPLE

Pre-event animation in schools and youth clubs helps to guarantee that the concerns and ideas of young people are fed into the collaborative planning process. Workshops can take place at schools, youth clubs and venues for after-school activities. Flexibility of approach is essential, along with seeking advice from youth leaders. An informal conversation with teenagers during their regular youth club session may be more appropriate than a formal workshop. Representatives from the school/youth groups should be encouraged to attend the charrette, report back their ideas and participate in the workshops. Outputs from working with young people, including their artwork, should be displayed and reported back at the public event.

Recent and exciting innovations involve running Minecraft workshops, where young people can work with a pre-constructed 3D computer model of the place and build interventions, working in teams or in groups, and even buddying with adults. The results of the work can then be collated and completed by the facilitator and displayed online or live at an event. This Minecraft gaming replicates some of the collaborative and iterative working processes that are such an important element of charrettes.

CONTACTING THE HARD-TO-REACH

A community includes many people who will be unlikely to attend an organised public event, due to health issues, age or personal circumstances, so making arrangements to meet such people in a reassuring and familiar environment will ensure wide participation in the engagement process. Informal meetings and one-to-one conversations can be arranged with hard-to-reach members of the community, such as the elderly and disabled, parents and toddlers and minority ethnic groups. Opportunities for informal discussions are likely to be found at lunch clubs, coffee mornings and regular sessions organised by churches and other religious and community groups.

INFORMATION COLLATION

The facilitation team will need information and technical materials, depending on the project, which may include site plans, topography and utilities information, land ownership plans, asset lists, aerial photographs, easements, regulatory requirements, historical mapping, precedent studies, building typologies or planning status.

THE CHARRETTE

Charrettes are referred to by a variety of names, and the exact methodology used depends on the practitioner facilitating the event, and what is felt to be appropriate for the particular place and process. The case studies in the next chapter will showcase a range of processes tailored to their specific community and project. The generic charrette programme that follows is based on the JTP Community Planning Weekend methodology, which puts community workshops upfront and ends with a final report-back presentation to the community of a vision for the future. It contains the key ingredients used by other processes, but perhaps in a different order and with different emphases.

To help explain the generic methodology, images from a real-life project have been selected. St Clement's Hospital is a curtilage-listed site and a former workhouse infirmary in Bow, East London. In 2012, the Mayor of London decided to establish London's first Community Land Trust (CLT) on the site. Galliford Try Linden Homes was selected as the GLA's development partner. The St Clement's Hospital Community Planning Workshop was held over two days, and more than 350 local people joined in to help create a vision for the delivery of 250 new homes. In late 2013 the scheme received unanimous approval from Tower Hamlets for detailed planning, listed building consent and conservation area consent.

PROGRAMME

It is important that charrette teams and facilitators adopt and evolve programmes and processes that they feel comfortable with, but which still fulfil the main principles and functions of a charrette.

EXAMPLE FIVE-DAY CHARRETTE

The length and timing of a charrette may vary to suit local circumstances. The following example is of a typical five-day charrette process to show what can be covered. A five-day charrette will give the community ample opportunity to participate and facilitate team working to analyse the outcomes, and draw up and present the resulting vision to the community to the required quality and detail. Charrettes have also been successfully held for shorter periods, for example the Barnes Ponder in Chapter 5, and so a simple shorter programme has also been included to illustrate this approach.

The charrette should be held at an appropriate accessible venue. This will vary depending on the project, but could be a village hall, a school, or a civic or community building. Generally, for logistical reasons one venue is preferred, but it may be appropriate or necessary to hold different stages of the process in different venues.

The event should be held at times when people can participate fully, to ensure that as broad a cross-section of the community as possible can attend and take part. It is beneficial to provide childcare and to ensure full accessibility, including installing a hearing loop system.

The timing of the charrette must suit the local situation and should be agreed by the steering group and the

EXAMPLE FIVE DAY CHARRETTE PROGRAMME

DAY ONE - FRIDAY Team briefing Public workshops	**Morning** – Team walkabout and technical briefing. Venue set up.
	Afternoon and evening – Public session. Background exhibition, workshops, hands-on planning groups and walkabouts, including young people's workshop organised through schools and possible local business workshop. Groups will assess options and develop ideas and report back to the plenary session.
DAY TWO - SATURDAY Public workshops Team dinner	**Morning and afternoon** – Public session. Workshops, hands-on planning groups and site walkabouts/investigations. Groups will assess options and develop ideas and report back to the plenary session. Way forward workshop.
	Evening – Team dinner.
DAYS THREE & FOUR - SUNDAY & MONDAY Team working	**Day and evening** – Team working.
DAY FIVE - TUESDAY Team working Report back	**Day** – Team working.
	Evening – Report back. PowerPoint presentation and exhibition for the community.

facilitation team. Consideration should be given to the needs of various groups; for example, organised participation of school children is usually easier during school hours, and local traders may find evening sessions most convenient. Charrettes are typically held on consecutive days but it may be necessary or appropriate to tailor charrettes in a different sequence due to venue availability or other requirements of the charrette.

The public workshops feed into the team's analysis and

ALTERNATIVE SHORT CHARRETTE PROGRAMME

DAY ONE - FRIDAY	Walkabout and briefing. Venue set up.
DAY TWO - SATURDAY	Background exhibition, public session – workshops, hands-on planning groups and walkabouts, including young people's workshop organised through schools and possible local business workshop. Groups will assess options and develop ideas and report back to the plenary session. Way forward workshop.
Interim days	Team working away from venue.
One or two weeks later	Evening – Report back. PowerPoint presentation and exhibition for the community.

FIGURE 4.3:
Background exhibitions like this one at St Clement's are important to share knowledge with the local community, and provide an information point for those who only want to drop in for a short while

design working stages, when the project team draws consensus from the community input, and brings this together in the form of a public presentation on the final day of the charrette.

MEETING AND GREETING
The role of team members at reception is very important. Their role is to make participants feel welcome, explain what is happening and collect names and addresses on sign-in sheets. All team members should have team badges, and name badges can be created for participants using address labels.

BACKGROUND EXHIBITION AND COMMENT FORMS
A background exhibition is useful for briefing, and provides a place for one-to-one discussions with people who may not want to participate in a workshop session. Material displayed may include an introduction to the project and charrette team, plans showing the place or site location and highways network, some urban design analysis, landscape and ecology information and historic maps and data describing how a place has changed over time.

It is important for team members to be on hand to answer questions, capture points of view and encourage people to come back to the final presentation.

Comment forms should be provided for people to write down their views and ideas.

STICKY-NOTE DIALOGUE WORKSHOPS
The workshop facilitator initiates a simple group activity, which first identifies the issues, then looks at possible opportunities and how best these can be implemented. Participants contribute their suggestions by jotting them down on sticky notes, which are then gathered in by the facilitators and grouped to identify key themes. Ideas are discussed as they arise, enabling a full dialogue between all participants in a fully inclusive process.

At St Clement's
dialogue workshops
were held at the
beginning of each
public day to
understand local
issues regarding
the proposed
development, and
aspirations for
change. The use
of sticky notes
allows for broad
participation and
significant ground
to be covered in a
short time

Guided site visits to
St Clement's enabled
participants to
experience first-hand
the qualities of the
site and consider the
opportunities for its
regeneration

The combination of written ideas and professional
facilitation allows the ideas of the less confident to
be placed on an equal footing with those of the more
experienced. The process also reduces the potential for
aggressive and single-issue dissent. While the workshops
encourage local people to express their views, it is
important for 'professionals' and the presentation
'providers' to be on hand to give information and join
the debate.

Typical questions may include:

- Where the project sits within the planning process
- Who owns the site
- What the expectations are in terms of the amount of
  development of the site, for example the amount and
  type of uses proposed
- Technical and engineering issues such as water,
  flooding and sewerage
- Green space and environmental issues
- Projected start date and completion date for the
  project

TOURS AND WALKABOUTS

As a charrette is held in the place under consideration,
it provides a good opportunity for the community and the
facilitation team to view key sites together, so that each
can learn from the other. Bus tours of the place and the
surrounding area form part of the initial team briefing,
and walkabouts during the workshop sessions can help
with the understanding of issues and opportunities and
inspire creative solutions.

HANDS-ON PLANNING SESSIONS

These sessions provide the opportunity for participants
to explore the physical implications of the ideas that
have already emerged through the topic/dialogue
workshops. Several small groups work simultaneously
with members of the facilitation team around large-scale
maps, which enables the group to develop their ideas in
an informal session. Models can be used too, but at the
initial stage drawings are more flexible and effective in
developing concepts.

Typical group themes include The Big Picture, Landscape

FIGURE 4.6:
Facilitated hands-on planning groups working around plans of the site and the surrounding area were able to explore constraints, opportunities and options for the regeneration of St Clement's. Each group focused on a different topic and reported back their ideas to a plenary session

and Open Space, Getting About, Community Amenities, Principles of Sustainability, Scheme Layout, and so on. The topics under consideration may relate to the area as a whole, or to some small part of it.

The results are recorded in a visual form and each group explains their ideas to everyone present in a plenary report back session. The group report back presentations should be given by participants rather than facilitators where possible. Facilitators may add further input if something is missed, or clarification of a technical point if it is judged to be helpful. The 'visuals' from each hands-on-planning session are then displayed and form part of the expanding exhibition.

Holding more than one hands-on planning session during a charrette enables ideas to be developed and fed back in an iterative process. These feedback loops are important for developing the proposals and building understanding and consensus.

WAY FORWARD WORKSHOP
Having asked local people to take part in a collaborative planning exercise, it is important to discuss the next steps with the community through a way forward workshop. Discussion topics may include how the process will continue, how people can stay informed, and how early projects that might have emerged can be taken forward.

It is important to continue the momentum and sense of common ownership built up during the charrette.

TEAM WORKING
In a five-day collaborative process, the facilitation team and consultants then work together during the next three days to analyse and evaluate the outputs from the two days of public participation. The workshop data is summarised and the hands-on planning drawings photographed and given an explanatory key.

Distillation of written and drawn material will result in a number of key themes, which reflect the overall concerns and suggestions raised by members of the community.

An illustrative vision or masterplan is drawn up, using ideas generated during the workshops and hands-on planning sessions.

A presentation is put together, with slides showing what happened during the charrette, and including background information, useful precedents, and details of how those who attended the public event have influenced the design.

REPORT BACK PRESENTATION
The report back on Day Five will draw out points of consensus, identify potential dilemmas, provide a

BELOW FIGURE 4.7:
Through the development of the proposals for St Clement's, regular Community Forums were held to update the community and give them the opportunity to comment on the emerging plans

historical overview, and present the illustrated vision including an indicative masterplan and action plan.

A printed newsletter can also be produced for distribution to the community following the report back, setting out the key outcomes and including the vision or masterplan.

OUTPUTS

The charrette process can become a springboard to help implement future development. Outputs can be used in a variety of ways according to the aims and objectives of the project.

The result of a vision-building design process may form the basis of a Local Plan or development masterplan for an area, or for a specific site. It can help solve critical decisions about town-wide regeneration, or assist in implementing a town-planning strategy. It can initiate the setting up of collaborative mechanisms,

such as Community Development or Community Land Trusts, through which a development can be delivered. The main output of participation in planning is that contributors to the process have shared ownership of the plan that is produced.

Support for development-led economic growth at a local level requires the involvement and commitment of people who recognise and respond to a shared vision. Using a compressed timescale and the benefits of open dialogue, a practical way forward is usually found, held together by a sense of collective ownership of an overarching vision, which many people have helped to create. In this way all stakeholders, whether representing the local government, the community or the private sector, will have collaborated in exploring the complexities of future change, and in helping to create a place that they will all share.

DEVELOPMENT OF PROPOSALS

The community should be kept actively involved as the development proposals progress. This can be through ongoing Community Forum meetings, exhibitions, newsletters and 'Learning from Elsewhere' visits. The project website and social media should be updated regularly to make sure as many people as possible are kept informed about the proposals. Community Forum meetings provide the opportunity for professionals, such as highways consultants, to explain the finer details of the plans as they develop.

SUSTAINING LOCAL INVOLVEMENT

A Community Forum or Town Team with subsidiary working groups can follow as a direct result of a charrette process. This will help bind the community together in a realistic, politically open and democratic way. Once a vision has been created, partnering arrangements can then be set up with the relevant stakeholders to oversee delivery. Out of this new process new leaders and community champions may emerge. In some places, 'meanwhile' or interim uses have been brought into the

FIGURE 4.8:
At St Clement's the community were keen to signal the regeneration of the site through activities and events. Soon after the planning weekend a huge bow was made and mounted on the clock tower to herald the changes to come. This was followed by two hugely successful cultural festivals organised by Shuffle, a new not-for-profit organisation, now based in the nearby Cemetery Park

site as a signal for regeneration and to bring more active uses into the site over time. In others, new community-based structures have been created, such as Town Teams, Community Development Trusts and Community Land Trusts, which can have a long-term impact on delivery. Other forms of community based organisations which can deliver and manage projects for the benefit of the community include parish councils, cooperatives, Building Preservation Trusts and Community Interest Companies.

TOWN TEAMS

A Town Team is a non-political and unelected grouping made up of a wide range of local community interests and stakeholders, including the local business community, who meet to develop and deliver collaborative and strategic plans for their area. In some cases, Town Teams have been set up with a wider remit covering the whole town, and have been given power to help decide how incoming public regeneration funds are spent.

COMMUNITY DEVELOPMENT TRUSTS

Private, public sector and community interests can be combined through transferring land and assets to a Community Development Trust. This will then create an active, stabilising force that can operate effectively, regardless of political change. The public sector provides the legal framework, the market provides the finance to set up appropriate partnerships, and the community becomes a long-term stakeholder.

COMMUNITY LAND TRUSTS

A Community Land Trust enables land to be secured and kept in community ownership in perpetuity, passed down through the generations. Community Land Trusts can be set up to deliver permanently affordable housing, ensuring that people are not priced out of their neighbourhoods. Houses can be sold or rented at a rate that is linked to local incomes. Membership of the Trust can be open to anyone who lives, works or has strong active ties to a social institution in the area.

DESIGN CODES

A design code (or form-based code) regulates land development to deliver a specific urban form to ensure predictable results and high-quality public realm as a way of organising the development. The codes are advocated as a way of ensuring that the results of the collaborative planning process are written into the planning consents, so that agreed principles are not watered down by those who eventually deliver the development.

EVALUATING THE OUTCOMES

Once a process starts delivering results, it is important to evaluate the outcomes. This can help identify successful and less-successful initiatives and adjust future activities, and should also help with applying for funding or entering awards. The knowledge will also help on other projects and feed into the wider body of knowledge about the collaborative planning process.

Aerial drawing of the vision for
Scarborough's renaissance

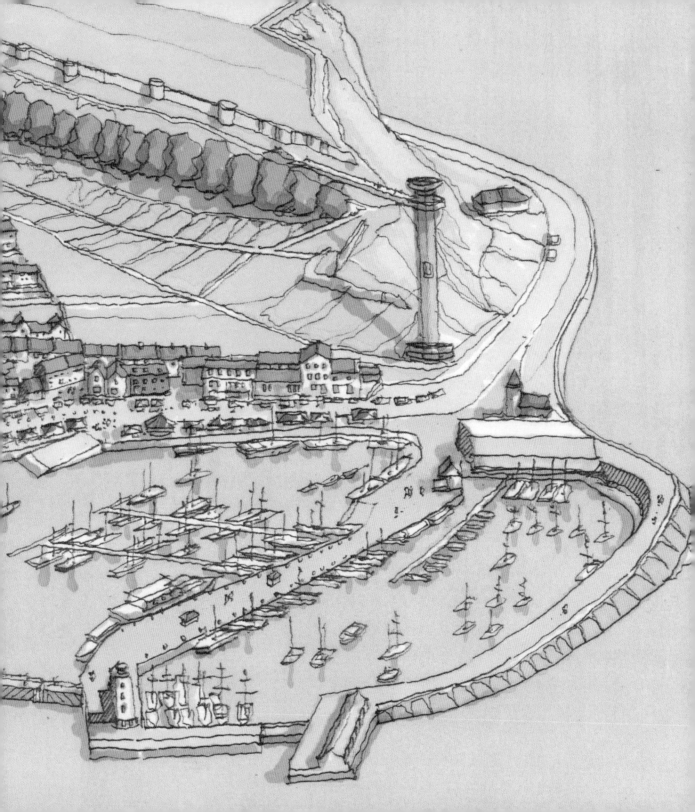

5.1

5.3

5.4

5.9

5.10

5.13

CHAPTER | 5

20|20 CASE STUDIES

5.6   5.7   5.8

5.14   5.17   5.19

INTRODUCTION

This chapter focuses on twenty international case studies chosen to illustrate a broad spectrum of places and communities around the world where a charrette process has been used.

All the processes are related to change. They offer communities a way to express concerns and ideas, which are then considered by the charrette team and reinterpreted as valued and effective inputs: people's views are heard and honoured.

The case studies demonstrate that charrettes can give people more control over changes to their community and environment. Feelings can often change too – from negative and passive to positive and proactive.

In many instances, the processes have resulted in huge learning curves for the professionals and politicians involved, and in some cases they have changed lives and careers. There are examples of communities getting involved in the pre-charrette organisational phase and the post-charrette delivery phase, whose members then go on to manage and deliver buildings and services. This is in addition to involvement in the charrette itself.

I have worked on many of the charrettes featured in the case studies, collaborating with colleagues from JTP and other practices. For case studies I have not been involved in personally, I am indebted to colleagues for directing me towards selected processes in their parts of the world, and for providing images and text.

While writing this book, I have returned to some places, and visited others for the first time, to assess outcomes from the charrettes and talk to participants. Most quotations come from personal conversations or from telephone conversations with people who participated in the original events.

What has become evident is the clarity of thinking and purpose that was developed through the charrette processes. This was affirmed by the communities and professionals involved. Apart from the tangible delivery of some truly inspiring projects, perhaps the most valuable result has been the relationships that developed within the communities themselves, which has led to further successes that would never otherwise have happened.

The case studies show that communities should not be feared, but welcomed as key participants in planning at any scale, as their input will help deliver what is right and best for the community concerned.

The case studies are presented in three sections: Foresight, Vision and Hindsight. Foresight explains the background to the place and why a charrette was decided on. Vision explains the process and the resulting vision, or masterplan. Hindsight looks back at the charrette from today's perspective and assesses what has happened since. The final chapter of the book considers the case studies together and draws out the lessons learned.

To give an overview of the case studies and to enable the reader to select charrettes that are of most interest to them, a matrix is included. The charrettes are categorised by location and date, with category headings as follows.

CLIENT SECTOR

Depending on the body that initiated the charrette process, they are differentiated as 'Public', 'Private' or 'Community'/Third. Public sector includes local authorities, non-governmental agencies and national governments. Private includes private landowners, land promoters or masterplan developers, or developers who will go on to build out the resulting scheme. Community/Third includes civic or charitable bodies or community groups. In the latter case, raising funds to involve professional facilitators can be a key challenge.

SCALE

The 'Regional' category includes charrettes that cover more than one distinct settlement and deal with connections and infrastructure. 'City/Town' charrettes may involve a whole settlement, or part of a settlement such as a town centre that is significant enough to warrant engaging the whole settlement community. 'Neighbourhood' is more localised and typically covers a site or area that can be treated as a distinct development or regeneration opportunity, and which impacts on people within walking distance from the site.

SITE

Most of the charrettes are held in the context of an existing Urban, settlement, be it a city, town or village. The 'Rural' category describes a site set in the countryside or bush, distinct from the nearest settlement.

VISION FOCUS

This category describes the primary professional or subject discipline that is the focus of the charrette — some charrettes fall into more than one category.

The 'Planning' category has a strategic focus, which will impact on future planning policy of the particular local community or local government.

'Urban design' involves a finer-grained focus that considers land use, layout and the relationship between streets and spaces. 'Green design' includes charrettes that have a landscape and/or environmental focus.

The 'Architecture' category includes the design of buildings and their relationships with place. And finally, 'Governance' refers to community involvement being designed in to decision making in relation to delivery and future management of the place.

CASE STUDIES

	CASE	COUNTRY	CHARRETTE DATE	
5.1	SANTA FE	US	February 1997	
5.2	BELFAST	Northern Ireland	February 1997	
5.3	PERTH	Australia	September 1997	
5.4	CATERHAM	England	February 1997	
5.5	NASHVILLE	US	July 1999	
5.6	SCARBOROUGH	England	April 2002	
5.7	REYKJAVIK	Iceland	November 2004	
5.8	VANCOUVER	Canada	April 2005	
5.9	LIVERPOOL	England	September 2005	
5.10	KEW BRIDGE, LONDON	England	July 2006	
5.11	LÜBECK	Germany	March 2007	
5.12	DUBLIN	Ireland	November 2007	
5.13	BLAENAU FFESTINIOG	Wales	October 2008	
5.14	DUNEDIN	New Zealand	June 2011	
5.15	WICK AND THURSO	Scotland	February 2012	
5.16	DUMFRIES	Scotland	September 2012	
5.17	CADDINGTON	England	April 2013	
5.18	BARNES, LONDON	England	October 2013	
5.19	LIANGZHU	China	June 2015	
5.20	PADDINGTON, LONDON	England	May 2016	

CLIENT SECTOR			SCALE			SITE		VISION FOCUS				
PUBLIC	PRIVATE	COMMUNITY/THIRD	REGION	CITY/TOWN	NEIGHBOURHOOD	URBAN	RURAL	PLANNING	URBAN DESIGN	GREEN DESIGN	ARCHITECTURE	GOVERNANCE
●		●			●	●			●	●		●
●					●	●			●			
●				●		●		●	●			
	●				●	●			●			●
●					●	●		●	●			
●				●		●		●	●			●
	●				●		●	●	●	●		
	●				●	●			●	●		
●				●		●		●	●	●		
	●				●	●			●		●	
●		●		●		●			●			
●					●	●		●	●			
●		●		●		●			●			
●					●	●			●			
●			●	●		●		●	●			
●					●	●			●	●		
					●	●			●	●		
		●			●	●			●			●
	●			●		●						●
		●			●	●			●			

SANTA FE RAILYARD REGENERATION
SANTA FE, NEW MEXICO, US

DATE **FEBRUARY 1997** CLIENT SECTOR **PUBLIC/THIRD** SITE **URBAN** SCALE **NEIGHBOURHOOD**
VISION **URBAN DESIGN GREEN DESIGN GOVERNANCE**

What to do with a large, valuable railyard that becomes available in the heart of the historic, thriving state capital of New Mexico – who decides?

'The oral history of Santa Fe goes back 200 years or more, way before the railway, so local people have much longer-term thinking, back into the past and forward into the future. We are now twenty-five to thirty years on from when the city bought the property, but that is just a blip in time for a 400-year-old city. I am very gratified by the way the community has adopted the railyard as their own space.'

Steve Robinson, President of Santa Fe Railyard Community Corporation

FORESIGHT

Santa Fe, founded by the colonial Spanish in 1610, is the oldest state capital in the US. The indigenous Pueblo people had previously inhabited the land, living in small village settlements over thousands of years. The 'modern' city, set at the foot of the Sangre de Cristo Mountains on the edge of the Rockies, has an altitude of more than 2,100 m (7,000 ft) and a cooler climate than the surrounding lower-lying desert. It is a fashionable and highly liveable city,

characterised by attractive adobe buildings in the historic downtown. It has a burgeoning arts and culture scene, which makes it a popular place for both visitors and residents.

In the late nineteenth century, the Santa Fe Railyard was built on agricultural land irrigated by the Acequia Madre ('mother ditch'). In 1880 the first train arrived at Santa Fe station, and for over 100 years the yard was a vibrant commercial and tourist hub, a focal point for the town. Almost overnight, however, the opening of the interstate highway made the railyard practically obsolete. Depending on the time of year it was either a mud pit or a dustbowl.

The 1980s was a time of significant growth for Santa Fe, and the railway land, being close to the city centre, became very valuable. Inevitably the Atchison, Topeka and Santa Fe Rail Company decided to develop the site. Discussions between the city government and the rail company led to the creation of a masterplan, drawn up in Boston, which proposed tearing up the rail tracks, demolishing the buildings and constructing one and a half million square feet of real estate.

Local architect Suby Bowden recalls that the plan was first seen at a council design review. The railway put up a for sale sign, and there was 'uproar in the community, who saw it as their land'. Steve Robinson, President of the Santa Fe Railyard Community Corporation, agrees: 'There was a strong sense of sadness – is this is what our heritage has come to – another faux-adobe shopping mall and a hotel?'

Eventually there was so much opposition that the masterplan was abandoned. This gave Suby the opportunity to go to the city council and suggest an alternative, more culturally sensitive approach.

At that time the town plaza was being taken over by tourists, and the community needed their own space. A concept emerged in which the plaza would be the 'living room'

for guests, and the railyard would become a focus for families and local people, with a park and weekly community activities. The next bold step was for the Trust for Public Land to acquire the land and hold on to it until they were sure that a park could actually be built. The city eventually bought the property from the Trust in 1995 and then began the process of its conversion into a public, mixed-use development.

Having discarded the masterplan proposal, discussions took place locally about how to set up a community-based planning process, and Gayla Bechtol, from the local AIA chapter, suggested an R/UDAT. The concept that citizens would be consulted was unprecedented in Santa Fe, which had a 'patron' system going back 400 years.

Expertise and free advice is a positive element of R/UDATs, but some local people were concerned that if experts came in to design the railyard, it would discourage participation by the community. It was therefore decided to run ten or twelve months of community-based planning, followed by the R/UDAT.

Weekly public meetings took place over six months in 1996, to which anyone could bring their ideas. It was a process of simply listening to the community and discussing what land uses people wanted in the railyard, and what the priorities were.

During this time, an R/UDAT steering group was set up to organise the charrette, with a wide range of members including the local AIA chapter, the City Planning Department, the Santa Fe Land Use Resource Center, the Trust for Public Land and the Metropolitan Redevelopment Commission. Suby recollects that 'there were lots of women in top positions – it was a female-led process which believed you could collaborate'.

VISION
The charrette was held over three weekends in February 1997. The first weekend focused on a design workshop facilitated by local

designers. One hundred and twenty citizens signed up for the whole weekend. This was followed by a citizen vote to determine land uses, which fed into the R/UDAT on the second weekend.

The R/UDAT was an intense and creative 'window' within a long, drawn-out planning process. The team, led by Charles M Davis, FAIA, included ten volunteer advisors from outside Santa Fe. Members of the team went on town and site tours and did many interviews. They then focused on creating a community plan, which had sections on governance, implementation, planning and transportation, as well as finance. The plan enabled people to visualise what the area might be like in the future, and it also gave the city council information about financial commitments.

On the fourth night of the R/UDAT the local newspaper published the results in a special edition, which was distributed to the whole town.

During the third weekend, the town's citizens came together to discuss principles from the R/UDAT proposals and to ratify the plan. By that time many of the same people were attending all the meetings – so, with the benefit of the widespread distribution of the newspaper, a telephone survey was conducted. This revealed 75 per cent support for the proposals among the wider community. Subsequently, the councillors unanimously adopted the plan.

Seven thousand people (over 10 per cent of the population) actively participated in a year of public participation through surveys, questionnaires and meetings.

HINDSIGHT
The masterplan and design code for the railyard were completed in 2001. 'Meanwhile uses' included outdoor activities, such as movies in the park and a farmers' market. The city council originally offered to manage the park, but the community eventually took it over on a ninety-year lease. An international competition was held for the park and piazza, which was won by a landscape and urban design team headed by Ken Smith, Frederic Schwartz and Mary Miss. The design concepts focused on the

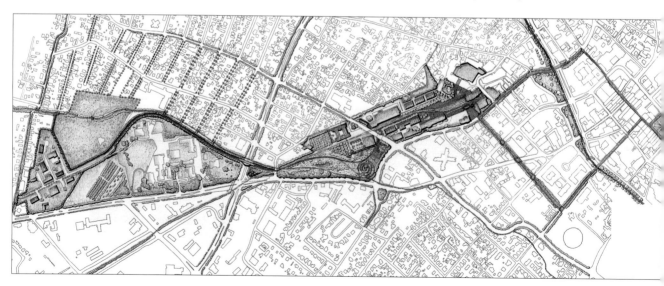

ABOVE LEFT FIGURE 5.1.4:
Santa Fe Railyard Park

ABOVE RIGHT FIGURE 5.1.5:
Santa Fe farmers' market

railway aesthetic, indigenous planting and respect for the Acequia Madre, which runs through the site.

The pace of building and refurbishment was slow, but finally in 2008 came the grand opening of the 4-hectare (10-acre) park and piazza. Industrial buildings had been restored for local business use, and new buildings were in operation. A commuter train service was established, and 10,000 people turned out to celebrate the arrival of the first train from Albuquerque.

The public involvement process still continues through the management of the award-winning park, which is run according to four values: time, culture, land and oral history. In 2017 an impressive ninety-six public events were held in the park.

The Santa Fe Railyard Community Corporation, created out of the R/UDAT process, now offers low rates and rents for businesses, and is developing low-cost housing to the west end of the site.

The regular Saturday farmers' market is thronged with locals and visitors, and traders are delighted with the facilities laid on for them. For one shopper, the Santa Fe Railyard is now 'the new downtown – it's where you come to socialise ... you can purchase something from a vendor ... next thing you know you've been talking for twenty minutes'.

Those fighting for their land came from a largely Hispanic background. The farmers were the connection between the land and its agricultural past, and the city's roots lie in an oral rather than a written tradition. As Suby Bowden says, 'Santa Fe has a long memory. Perhaps, as a consequence, it moves slowly and is OK with that'. Gayla Bechtol concludes: 'I am most proud of the democracy that happened – helping people have a voice that otherwise wouldn't have a voice in the process; that was for me the most gratifying – it was just cool.'

A FIRST STEP FOR THE CRUMLIN ROAD

BELFAST, NORTHERN IRELAND

DATE **FEBRUARY 1997**   CLIENT SECTOR **PUBLIC**   SITE **URBAN**
SCALE **NEIGHBOURHOOD**   VISION FOCUS **URBAN DESIGN**

A community planning process was used to take a tentative first step to create common ground between two communities in conflict, by agreeing acceptable uses along the high road they share.

'Unless you were from the area you never knew when you passed from one community to the other. It was a real patchwork and very difficult to get agreement on major regeneration projects.'

Tony McCusker, Head of Regeneration, Department of the Environment

ABOVE FIGURE 5.2.1:
British Army mobile patrol along the Crumlin Road during the Troubles, 1971

FORESIGHT

Crumlin Road is an interface between the Protestant and Catholic communities of North Belfast. For thirty years it was synonymous with the Troubles, featuring regularly on news bulletins around the world reporting a seemingly endless series of attacks and murders. Even after the Good Friday Agreement of 1998, the Crumlin Road was in the headlines again in August 2000 when two loyalists associated with Ulster Defence Association brigadier Johnny Adair were shot and killed while sitting in their jeep.

Crumlin Road is one of Belfast's key arterial routes, linking the city to the Antrim Hills and beyond. Historically, the route connected some of the city's principal linen mills to the city centre and the docks, and thousands of jobs in manufacturing and shipbuilding sustained the area's economy. The road is also known for being the location of many significant buildings, such as the Mater Hospital, Crumlin Road Gaol and Crumlin Road Courthouse. As well as churches and community buildings, there are mills, shops and homes along the road.

By 1996 the Crumlin Road had seen thirty years of decline and neglect due to the Troubles, the waning of Belfast's economy, especially in shipbuilding, and the blight of a planned but unrealised road widening scheme. As well as being the site of some of the city's worst dereliction, the Crumlin Road area was also one of the most deprived in the city.

Housing and territory have long been key issues in North Belfast. The Protestant areas have been depopulating while the Catholic

ABOVE FIGURE 5.2.2:
Aerial photo along the Crumlin Road looking west to the Antrim Hills

population is growing and requires more space for housing, but the former community would not concede to the latter.

Making Belfast Work (MBW) was launched in 1988 by the Northern Ireland Department of the Environment, to strengthen and target more effectively the efforts being made by the community, the private sector and the government to address the economic, educational, social, health and environmental problems facing local people.

In the mid-1990s MBW decided to focus on the regeneration of Belfast's arterial routes. The intention was to bring marginalised communities into engagement with public authorities by building on a sense of optimism, encouraged by a new era of ceasefire.

VISION

In September 1996 John Thompson & Partners (JTP) was appointed to undertake a community planning process to develop a consensus vision for the future of the Crumlin Road. At the time it was seen as a dangerous road, with highly demarcated territory and with no sense of free movement. By bringing the two communities together and focusing on a road they both used, MBW hoped that some compromise and agreement might emerge.

A key objective was to find future uses for the gaol and courthouse, both designed by architect Sir Charles Lanyon, and built in the mid-nineteenth century. Since the declaration of a ceasefire in 1995, these listed buildings stood vandalised and unused, facing each other across the Crumlin Road. MBW was seeking new uses for them both but needed the permission of the community.

The initial aim was to hold a publicly advertised 'community conference', with the potential to produce a 'community plan'. However, following preparatory work in Stage One, community leaders believed this proposal to be too prescriptive and potentially divisive.

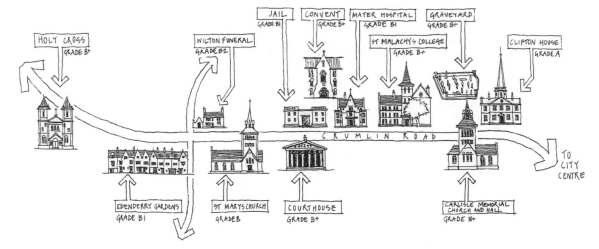

A steering committee was formed to oversee the preparation of the event, under the chairmanship of Jonathan Davis, then a director at JTP. The practice was viewed as a trusted and neutral party, and it was important not to force the timetable.

A critical role of the steering committee was for the representatives of both the nationalist and loyalist communities to meet and broker a mutually acceptable venue, agenda and format for the event. Intense discussions ensued during which the process was debated and sometimes put in doubt. An agreed position was eventually worked out, which provided clear definitions of what the process sought to achieve, and what it did not. To do so, two lists were created as follows.

What the process IS:
- **A first step**
- **A flexible framework**
- **An opportunity for discussion and dialogue**
- **A way of focusing on a future vision**
- **A move towards sharing resources**
- **Positive 'coexistence'**
- **A way to identify areas of consensus**

What the process ISN'T:
- **A final outcome or masterplan**
- **An attempt to solve all the problems and conflicts**
- **Threatening the autonomy of different neighbourhoods**
- **Enforcing partnership**
- **A community relations exercise**
- **Engendering unnecessary conflict**

The event was redefined as an invitation-only 'Ideas Weekend' with the output to be a 'flexible framework' rather than a masterplan, which would form the basis for further discussions. As the agreed title of JTP's subsequent report stated, this was to be 'A First Step for the Crumlin Road'.

The Ideas Weekend took place over five days between 20 and 24 February 1997 at the Spires Conference Centre in central Belfast. On Day one, following a project briefing, the facilitation team walked the full length of the Crumlin Road from west to east – a walkabout that was pre-notified to the communities to ensure safe passage.

Over 100 people attended the event, and participants took part in 'future workshops', which discussed the multifaceted problems of the Crumlin Road and gave participants the opportunity to consider ideas for the area, how change might be brought about, and by whom. During design table sessions the future of the Crumlin Road's public buildings, the relationship between the various residential communities and improvements for the overall quality of the environment were explored. A 'way forward' workshop focused attention on viable next steps.

Following the two public days, the JTP team drew together conclusions and recommendations to provide a flexible framework for a possible way forward. The results were presented back to the weekend participants in a slideshow.

Four potential project clusters were identified, which separately or together could have the potential to contribute to the regeneration of the area. In line with the steering committee's objectives, it was stressed that these were examples of how regeneration might be achieved, and were a first step, not a final outcome.

HINDSIGHT
Considering the Ideas Weekend process took place over a year before the Good Friday Agreement of 10 April 1998, it was a significant achievement that the event took place at all. It reflected the efforts being made by many local people as part of the peace process of the mid-1990s.

The event seemed to create a shift of imagination among participants, enabling a fragmented and depressing landscape to be seen as a cluster of opportunities that had the potential to be exploited for the benefit of all.

RIGHT FIGURE 5.2.4:
Team walkabout on day one of the ideas weekend

Looking back at the process, Roisin McDonough, formerly of MBW, recalls: 'I was very enthused about the process; it gave people a very keen sense of what things could look and feel like. Building relationships was a good thing, and the process encouraged a participative and deliberative form of democracy – it was intelligent.' The use of co-design sketching techniques gave visual expression to participants' ideas, and illustrated practical means by which these could be achieved.

What the actual event did not do, as some had feared it might, was to derail the hard work and carefully developed relationships that had been established over the preceding months by the steering committee.

During the twenty years since the event, resources have been directed into the area, which has resulted in new development and regeneration, better environment management and a brighter feel. But Crumlin Road still suffers from underinvestment, and the core issues have not gone away: there are very high levels of deprivation, and housing is still off the agenda.

The 1997 collaborative event, with its strict ground rules, supported a growing awareness that interfaces could be created; an acceptance of the permanent physical divide between two communities.

Communities would be separated in a way that would maintain the peace, as long as the interfaces were based on common interest and also respected the symbols and expression of community traditions. For example, both communities agreed that retail and community uses were acceptable for interface land, but not housing, as this would be construed as a territorial move.

Consequently, in January 2016, after a decade of controversy about what should be done with the former Girdwood Barracks in North Belfast, a £11.7m community and leisure hub has opened, offering first-class leisure, community and education facilities.

The Ideas Weekend also identified the potential for investment in the Crumlin Road Gaol as a way to develop leisure, cultural and heritage opportunities, which could have significant tourist appeal. In May 2002, the report of the North Belfast Community Action Project team discussed the need for a large-scale physical regeneration project in North Belfast, and highlighted the potential of the former Crumlin Road Gaol. By the end of 2012 the prison had reopened its doors as a tourist attraction, business space and conference centre. While much of the building is still to be fully let to businesses, the museum has been successful in attracting visitors, among them many former inmates from both sides of the political divide.

BELOW FIGURE 5.2.5:
Crumlin Road project clusters

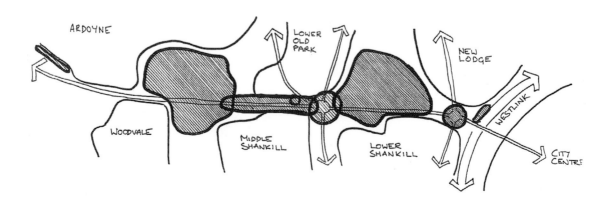

ABOVE FIGURE 5.2.6:
Crumlin Road Gaol today

Opposite the gaol, the courthouse, having suffered a number of fires in recent years and having failed to attract investment for adaptation and reuse has lain in a terrible state, a shadow of its former magnificence. But in March 2017 a Liverpool-based developer, Signature Living, bought the building with the intention of spending £25m to convert it into a 160-bedroom hotel, an initiative that has been supported by both sides of the community divide.

The Ideas Weekend was held at a critical time in Belfast's history, and it succeeded in bringing people together, building relationships and establishing agreed positions on many issues. A number of the identified physical projects have subsequently been delivered in a way that was jointly envisaged and agreed at the 1997 collaborative event.

Memories are still raw for many who live in this divided community, but the potential exists for further development that builds on the growing success of Northern Ireland's capital city. It is to be hoped that in the not-too-distant future political progress in Belfast will enable a new round of investment to be directed to key opportunity sites along the Crumlin Road, to everyone's benefit.

REVITALISING MIDLAND – A RAILWAY TOWN
PERTH, AUSTRALIA

DATE **SEPTEMBER 1997**   CLIENT SECTOR **PUBLIC**
SITE **URBAN**   SCALE **TOWN**   VISION **PLANNING   URBAN DESIGN**

Revisioning a former railway town has revived the spirit
of the community, formed a new creative economic base
and attracted investment to revitalise neighbourhoods and
landscapes.

'People still talk about the charrette twenty years later. They talk
about how capable, organised and intelligent the team members were,
and how they had a ready grasp of the data. They were very much
the servants of the community with the skills to interpret people's
aspirations.

Brian Hunt, local resident

ABOVE FIGURE 5.3.1:
**Heritage image of
Midland Railway
Workshops**

FORESIGHT

The township of Midland was established
in 1891 at the junction of two main highways
on the eastern fringes of Perth. Settlers had
occupied the privately owned land since the
1830s, but the arrival of the Midland Railway
Company in 1886 prompted its subdivision
and sale. In 1902 the Western Australian
Government Railway Workshops were
relocated from Fremantle to Midland, and the
rapidly expanding town was built on a history
of heavy engineering, with a fine tradition
of craftsmanship and innovation – skills that
were passed from generation to generation.

The Railway Workshops were vital to the
development and maintenance of the
Western Australian rail system, and a crucial
training ground for the skilled workforce of
some 4,000 people. A new rail station and
shopping centre were built in the early 1970s,
and the town's fortunes looked assured.

However, the closure of the Railway
Workshops in 1994 had an immediate and
devastating impact on Midland's local
economy and its multicultural community,
including European migrant workers. It was
not just the loss of their livelihoods, but also
their traditions, camaraderie and pride in
their work. Despite the best efforts of the
authorities, including locating government
and shire offices in the town centre, Midland
fell into sharp decline and the community's
morale suffered.

It was agreed by the City of Swan and the
Western Australia Ministry of Planning that
a community plan was needed to address
the complex and interrelated challenges
and opportunities. Ecologically Sustainable

ABOVE FIGURE 5.3.2:
Midland Revitalisation Charrette

BELOW LEFT FIGURE 5.3.3:
Plan of Railway Workshops redevelopment area

BELOW RIGHT FIGURE 5.3.4:
'Unleashing the giant' cartoon

Design (ESD), led by Chip Kaufman and Wendy Morris, was appointed to run a charrette process and develop integrated proposals, which could be implemented with the backing and involvement of the community.

VISION

The 'Midland Revitalisation Charrette' was held in 1997 with the support of a wide range of local bodies, to develop a strategy for this declining sub-regional centre and bring together a diverse group of stakeholders to craft a shared vision for the future of the town.

The charrette process ran for five days between 11 and 15 September 1997 at three locations in Midland. At each venue hundreds of local residents worked with the ESD team to consider the range of issues 'all at once'. During the first evening meeting, the mechanics of the charrette process were outlined and the local community had an opportunity to voice their concerns. Over the next days the multidisciplinary team collaborated intensively with local residents, including young people, businesses, landowners and government agencies, to explore and indicatively design opportunities and solutions.

On the concluding evening Chip Kaufman presented the illustrated vision for Midland's revitalisation. Design ideas and an economic strategy were presented for the whole of Midland, with the key focus on the heart of the town.

In addition, a range of proposals were presented for transport improvements in and around the town and the rehabilitation of the Helena River and Blackadder Creek. A key theme running through the presentation was an appreciation of the many assets of the town, and how they could be brought to the fore using the concept of 'unleashing the giant'.

From those few concentrated days of workshops and brainstorming emerged what became the blueprint for the transformation that followed. The charrette identified the growth areas of Swan View, West Stratton, Swan Park and Midland TAFE (Technical and Further Education) as places that had the potential to be strengthened with infill development, improved local centres, better linkages, and safer, more attractive streets, parks and environmental areas.

Key proposals for the heart of the redevelopment area included a 1-hectare (2.5-acre) oval of parkland, to be surrounded by 130 two-storey terraced houses, each with its own private front and rear gardens, and within easy walking distance of the town centre.

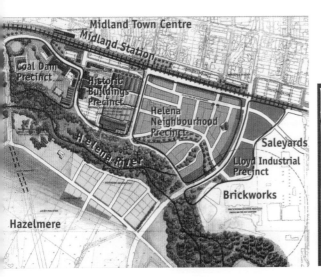

ABOVE FIGURE 5.3.5:
Sketch of ferry landing and marina at Woodbridge Landing

The charrette process enabled positive engagement with Aboriginal people who used to gather in a green space called Tuohy Gardens. This triangular street block with its confusing, uninviting pedestrian routes and hidden corners had become an ongoing problem area attracting antisocial behaviour. The charrette worked directly with the local Aboriginal community and proposed to solve all these problems by creating two new streets, redeveloping Tuohy Gardens as two-storey terraced housing, and by identifying a more suitable location nearby for Aboriginal gatherings and a cultural centre.

Following the charrette, the Shire President Councillor Charlie Gregorini was delighted that so many people embraced the potential for growth and development. He acknowledged that the City of Swan had set a new standard for how local government could work with its community in planning future growth in a sustainable manner.

Local resident Brian Hunt recalls: 'Midland had been languishing for some time, and people had come together at various times before to try to decide what to do and they produced nothing. The charrette was really helpful in stimulating a positive attitude in the community – they had skilled people that could sketch, draw and analyse but didn't preach.'

HINDSIGHT

Virtually all community groups supported the proposed charrette outcomes, including, most importantly, the Midland District's Chamber of Commerce and Industry. A steering committee was formed, with representation from the community and business groups and the council, which led to the state government establishing the Midland Redevelopment Authority (MRA) in 2000. This new agency was allocated land in the town centre, and the nearby 70-hectare (173-acre) Railway Workshops site, as the first stage of the redevelopment area.

Building on community ownership of the vision, the MRA has demonstrated an unwavering commitment to ensuring that the community continues to share and shape the charrette's dream and passion. Local communities and interest groups have been actively engaged in the project through further visioning exercises, forums, face-to-face liaison, local media, newsletters and reference groups. In particular, ESD were appointed to undertake another charrette in 2007 to review the process and outcomes and refresh the vision. Kieran Kinsella, CEO of the MRA, explains: 'I came to deliver the charrette outcomes, which had really strong community support. We need to keep true to the issues that came out and we keep refreshing our masterplan every four to five years – the people of the town continue to advocate for the things still to be done.'

New life has been breathed into cultural landmarks, such as the site of the Midland Railway Workshops, which is central to the area's sense of place. A new urban village has been created in the workshops precinct, with the retention and reuse of some of the original workshop buildings, and a mix of new residential, commercial, health, education and creative industry uses.

Located west of the site, Woodbridge Lakes has been developed as a new environmentally friendly, medium-density neighbourhood with attractive public spaces and parklands. There are

ABOVE FIGURE 5.3.6:
**Midland Workshops
Heritage Open Day**

committed affordable housing options to support a diverse population. Apartments and other higher-density dwellings are interspersed among parks, shops, cafes and transportation to provide an inner-city lifestyle. More than 150,000 square metres of new commercial and retail floor space has been created in the Clayton Street shopping hub, Midland Central.

The Midland Workshops Heritage Open Day, hosted by the Metropolitan Redevelopment Authority, was held on Sunday 8 September 2014 and gave local residents, former workers and the wider Perth community an opportunity to look inside the iconic buildings and celebrate this important heritage precinct.

Perhaps the greatest achievement of the MRA, and the principal reason for its success, has been the continuation of partnerships established at the time of the first charrette, which have been nurtured and maintained since by the various stakeholder groups. The organisations that helped formulate the concept plan for a revitalised Midland have remained active and enthusiastic participants in the process — not always in total agreement, but committed to realising a joint vision of a vibrant and exciting town.

Midland is now brimming with confidence as local investors, developers, businesses and residents commit to the continuing journey ahead, and have become a formidable army of ambassadors for the town.

REGENERATION OF A HISTORIC MILITARY BARRACKS
CATERHAM, SURREY, ENGLAND

DATE **FEBRUARY 1997**   CLIENT SECTOR **PRIVATE**   SITE **URBAN**   SCALE **NEIGHBOURHOOD**
VISION **URBAN DESIGN GOVERNANCE**

Collaborative masterplanning transformed a former army barracks into a popular and award-winning mixed-use village community.

'It's not just about the bricks and mortar — it's about people's lives, and building a community that gets on together well.'
Community Planning Weekend participant

ABOVE FIGURE 5.4.1:
Guards at Caterham

FORESIGHT
The Guards' Depot in Caterham, known as Caterham Barracks, was established in 1877 as the basic training establishment for the five regiments of Foot Guards, part of an elite personal bodyguard to the reigning monarch. Enclosed by a perimeter wall, the barracks included a Grade II listed chapel, designed by William Butterfield in 1885.

In 1960 the Guards' Depot transferred to Pirbright, and the barracks were used to accommodate various regiments. Many Guardsmen who had trained at the depot settled in Caterham after completing their service, and the local community was able to use the barracks facilities for sporting events, including boxing tournaments, and cricket and football matches. Sadly, this changed when security was tightened in August 1975, after an IRA bomb targeting soldiers exploded in a local pub. The barracks' closure in 1995 left a void in the community, and had a significant impact on the social and economic life of the town.

A local authority community consultation process in 1997 resulted in a planning brief with minimal built development (sixteen new houses plus the barrack blocks converted to residential) and unrealistic expectations regarding community amenities.

Although the brief was considered unviable by many developers, the site was bought by locally based Linden Homes. Linden recognised the local and historic importance of the barracks, and they were committed to delivering a high-quality neighbourhood. They also felt it was important to enable local residents and others to have a real

BELOW FIGURE 5.4.2:
**Drawing from one of
the hands-on planning
groups**

input into the evolution of proposals, and that additional development would be acceptable if significant community benefits were delivered, thereby creating a more dynamic and sustainable community.

Linden Homes appointed John Thompson & Partners (JTP) to create a masterplan for the site using a participatory process, including a 'Community Planning Weekend'. This marked the first time that a large-scale collaborative planning process had been promoted in the UK by a private developer.

VISION

The Caterham Barracks Community Planning Weekend took place in the NAAFI building between 27 February and 3 March 1998, and was attended by more than 1,000 people.

The event was structured around a combination of topic-based workshops, together with a large number of hands-on planning sessions, through which participants could discuss and actively contribute their design ideas. Teenagers from several local schools were involved, and local people could tour the barracks in a bus.

Over the course of the weekend a consensus emerged in favour of creating a balanced village community, including more than 360 homes (around 300 new-build) and a mix of uses set in a high-quality environment that respected the history of the site. New homes were laid out around the cricket green and on traditional street patterns. There were community facilities of a high standard, and green spaces managed by a new Community Trust.

Participants identified a number of possible community uses for existing buildings retained as part of the new neighbourhood, to be paid for by the increase in the number of homes provided on site. Uses for the buildings have, by and large, stood the test of time.

Local resident Marilyn Payne led the call for more facilities for young people, and within a few months 'Skaterham', a youth project providing skateboard, inline and BMX facilities, was set up in the former gymnasium. In March 2002 it transferred from the gymnasium to the listed chapel, and now has thousands of members.

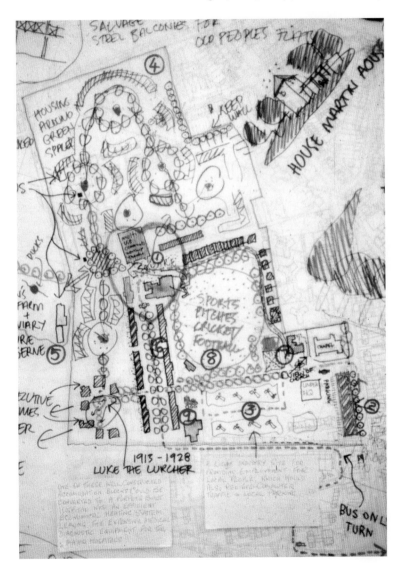

CATERHAM BARRACKS · AERIAL VIEW

TOP LEFT AND RIGHT FIGURES
5.4.3 & 5.4.3A:
**Guards marching out –
community 'guardians'
marching in cartoon**

CENTRE FIGURE 5.4.4:
**Vision for Caterham
Barracks – aerial drawing**

HINDSIGHT

The Community Planning Weekend marked the beginning of an ongoing process of collaboration between the community, the developers and the local authority, with the aim of creating a responsive new neighbourhood with a strong sense of place. A steering group was established to provide a forum for local residents, councillors and special interest groups. A number of specialist sub-groups met on over fifty occasions, involving over 100 local people. Ivan Ball, Linden's Project Director for redevelopment of Caterham Barracks, found himself spending more and more time working with the community. He subsequently moved into the village and became known as 'Mr Caterham'.

In due course, a series of recommendations were presented to Tandridge District Council with full community backing. The council changed its policy for the site and granted outline planning approval in June 1999, with the proposals delivered through a six-phase programme that was completed in 2008.

Governance of the new village at Caterham came about through the foundation of a Community Development Trust. This was the direct result of the Community Planning Weekend, during which local people expressed a desire for ongoing involvement in the creation and running of their community.

The village at Caterham was one of the first places to integrate private and affordable housing. The design of the affordable housing was indistinguishable from the private accommodation for sale, thereby achieving a genuine integration of tenure.

The Village has become known as a very healthy place to live, due to the provision of walking and cycle routes, and the access to open space. The 'Village Flyer' bus service began in September 2000, when the first residents moved in, to provide a transport link from the Village to Caterham railway station. Initially subsidised by Linden Homes, it is now funded through the residents' service charge.

BELOW FIGURE 5.4.5:
The Arc, Caterham

BOTTOM FIGURE 5.4.6:
**The Village at
Caterham – village
green**

The community planning process resulted in a highly viable development: over 360 new homes and millions of pounds' worth of community projects, including a nursery, a health and fitness centre, a swimming pool, a cricket pavilion, sports pitches, exhibition and rehearsal space, and an indoor skate park. The collaborative process and the resultant mixed-use development and community outcomes were researched and described in the publication 'Social Sustainability', published by JTP in 2013.

The success of the Village at Caterham has been recognised through numerous national and international awards, including the RTPI National Awards for Planning Achievement 2000 'Award for Planning for the Whole Community'. More importantly, it is the views of the community that have defined the development. An early resident of the converted barrack blocks emphasises the excitement of community collaboration: 'When you're in on the beginning of things – which is what the whole thing here was about – there is that sense of buzz and excitement. What's it going to turn out like? How much control will you have over it? Can you actually make it how you want it to be?'

And Ivan Ball concludes: 'It's just a fantastic scheme – you've got nice trees, nice old buildings, and it's a big enough site that we've been able to put in all the new facilities. I know I'm terribly biased, but if you're looking for a new home, this is as good as it gets.'

EAST NASHVILLE POST-TORNADO R/UDAT

NASHVILLE, TENNESSEE, US

DATE **JULY 1999** CLIENT SECTOR **PUBLIC** SITE **URBAN**
SCALE **NEIGHBOURHOOD** VISION **PLANNING** **URBAN DESIGN**

A consensus vision helped rebuild and revitalise a forgotten suburb, devastated by tornadoes in the 1930s and 1990s.

It was felt that the tornado could be a catalyst to take a downtrodden neighbourhood in decline and help make it better than it was before. The 1999 R/UDAT shaped my career as an architect – I became passionate about community planning.'

Hunter Gee, local architect

ABOVE FIGURE 5.5.1:
**The destructive
impact of the tornado
in East Nashville**

FORESIGHT

For many years East Nashville was a forgotten part of the city, located on 'the wrong side of the river'. This residential quarter had grown up in the early part of the twentieth century as a traditional, walkable neighbourhood of homes and community amenities, with local services at key junctions. Although it was separated from downtown Nashville by industrial land and the Cumberland River, the extensive network of trolley lines gave access to employment and services. Then a huge fire in 1916 and a tornado in 1933 damaged the area's vitality, and the building of the interstate highway encouraged the movement of the middle classes to the outer suburbs. From then on and for decades, East Nashville was largely ignored.

On 16 April 1998 another devastating tornado passed through Nashville's town centre and inner-city neighbourhoods, and East Nashville was worst hit. Local estate agent Cindy Evans describes the impact: 'The hurricane went downtown, broke office windows and then came across the river, and the restaurant where my friend worked had its roof blown off – she was blown from one room to another. Throughout the neighbourhood fallen trees were everywhere – you couldn't see the street. It's like we were hit by a bomb.' Most tellingly, Cindy concluded: 'It wasn't until late at night that the news said East Nashville had been hit – that's how inconsequential we were.'

The initial response to the tornado was impressive, with the East Nashville community and public sector pulling

ABOVE FIGURE 5.5.2:
Open-mic day at the R/UDAT

VISION

The multidisciplinary R/UDAT team was led by Bill Gilchrist and comprised nationally recognised land-use professionals from across the region, with backgrounds in landscape, housing, transport, venues and stadiums, community networking, urban design and management information systems.

The R/UDAT was held over four and a half days in July 1999. It started with a team tour of the area, followed by meetings with politicians and key stakeholders. Day two was an open-mic day at the Martha O'Bryan Center, where the team listened to local people who lined up to explain their likes, dislikes, needs and visions.

The location of the meetings was critical, to encourage a wide cross-section of the community to attend, and the open-mic session was programmed 'from 9am until the last person who has something to contribute'. Around 400 people were involved, and over 100 people spoke into the microphone.

Key themes to emerge included the value of having a diverse community and the need to ensure that regeneration did not force people out of the area. As well as the need for reconstruction following the tornado, other concerns raised included social services, greenway development, parks and playgrounds and crime prevention.

Participants stressed the need to attract people and better business to East Nashville, and residents said time and time again how they wanted the area to be restored to its original beauty and splendour.

Following the open-mic session, the R/UDAT team worked intensively, day and night, right up to the public report back presentation on Monday 19 July. One thousand people turned out to hear the outcomes from the charrette, which were presented using an overhead projector and transparencies.

together to clear streets, provide emergency help and restore services. Three months later, in July, Mayor Bredesen set up the Tornado Recovery Board, which decided to apply to the AIA to bring in an R/UDAT to create a plan for regeneration, simply because of its emphasis on community participation. It was felt that the tornado could be a catalyst to take a downtrodden neighbourhood in decline and help make it much better than it had been before. Carol Pedigo, one of the key forces behind bringing the R/UDAT to East Nashville, describes charrettes as: 'The best-kept secret – you're always better off with more ideas than just your own.'

In 1998 Hunter Gee was setting out on his career as an architect, and was very keen on community involvement. He was asked to chair the local steering committee, which included representatives of businesses, neighbourhood associations, public sector officials and councillors. The steering group raised the $50,000 to fund the R/UDAT and, as Hunter explains, 'one of the keys to success was the work we did over months to get the entire community represented – we spent many months building buy-in'.

LEFT FIGURE 5.5.3:
Sketch of a revitalised '100% corner' from the East Nashville R/UDAT

BELOW FIGURE 5.5.4:
Aerial sketch of Five Point, East Nashville

Three primary tasks were identified for the East Nashville community to undertake in order to enact the recommended changes. One was the need for community organisation. The second was a focus on developing public spaces and linkages. The third was the adoption of land-use policies that would enhance the unique character of this urban community.

The recommendations focused on the two major strengths of East Nashville that should be nurtured and receive investment, namely the diversity of the community which lay at the heart of the area's identity, and the essential quality and robustness of the urban fabric. The team identified the key importance of the commercial uses at road junctions within the neighbourhoods, and promoted these so-called '100% corners'.

HINDSIGHT
Hunter Gee recalls that the main recommendation was the creation

of a community council to oversee implementation of the R/UDAT's proposals. There was also a proposal to market the area and recognise that it had huge assets, such as the walkability of the neighbourhood.

A logo was created and a body established called 'Rediscover East', which still exists today. Rebuilding didn't happen overnight, of course: for ten years there were blue tarpaulins covering damaged buildings everywhere.

One thing Hunter would change about the process, if he could, would be the availability of funding for public infrastructure improvements: 'We could have found funding if we had staff – you need paid staff.' A couple of years later, some R/UDAT team members returned to East Nashville and challenged the city to invest in more staff for Rediscover East.

Hunter believes that the process of building the buy-in and holding the charrette set in motion a rising market that hasn't stopped, even to this day. East Nashville is now listed as one of the hippest neighbourhoods, which brings with it its own 'gentrification'

challenges, such as how to deliver affordable homes.

In 2012, building on an idea first discussed and sketched at the R/UDAT in 1999, the Metropolitan Development and Housing Agency announced the redevelopment of Cayce Place for 32 hectares (80 acres) of public housing. This meant tripling the density to enable bringing in mixed uses, including health provision. Smith Gee studio held a charrette attended by over 100 local stakeholders and citizens, and the resulting plan will deliver more than 2,300 new homes, open spaces and 20,000 m² (215,300 sq ft) of commercial and community uses.

Despite the successes and more recent acclaim for East Nashville, it's important to remember that the emotions and memories associated with the tornado's devastation have not been entirely forgotten. Cindy recalls: 'The tornado took down the huge sugar maples – when I drive home through these streets I can still remember how it used to be.'

ABOVE FIGURE 5.5.5:
Rediscover East logo

RIGHT FIGURE 5.5.6:
Revitalised and vibrant '100% corner' in East Nashville

TOWN IN DECLINE TO MOST ENTERPRISING PLACE

SCARBOROUGH, NORTH YORKSHIRE, ENGLAND

DATE **APRIL 2002**   CLIENT SECTOR **PUBLIC**   SITE **URBAN**   SCALE **TOWN**
VISION **PLANNING   URBAN DESIGN   GOVERNANCE**

The community of an iconic but declining seaside resort were empowered to create and proactively deliver a vision for the cultural and economic renaissance of their town.

'As a result of the process we have totally transformed our mindset and approach; we are much more enterprising and entrepreneurial – we can ring anyone in the town and make things happen.'

David Kelly, Scarborough's Head of Economic Development

FORESIGHT

At Scarborough, North Yorkshire, springs were discovered in the early seventeenth century, bubbling from the base of South Cliff on to the seashore. This marked the beginning of England's first seaside resort. Early visitors to the spa town were the aristocracy and landed gentry, who stayed for the summer season with their families and servants. The advent of the railways in the Victorian era led to the arrival of thousands

of day-trippers and holidaymakers, transforming the town's local economy and leading to the construction of large hotels on the seafront and a wide range of leisure attractions. Scarborough's expansion continued into the first part of the twentieth century, with municipal initiatives creating 142 hectares (350 acres) of public parkland. New housing estates were built on the outskirts of the town, and light industry arrived in the form of coach-building, printing, food-processing and engineering businesses.

However, Scarborough's fishing industry was in steady decline, and from the 1970s tourism also started to suffer, due to the growing popularity of package holidays to the Mediterranean. By the end of the twentieth century the town seemed unable to halt the decay and dereliction that was steadily eroding the assets of this once-splendid place.

Scarborough's geographical isolation, which had originally been part of its attraction, became a distinct threat. Its relatively poor road and rail links to York, the nearest city, meant that people quipped about it being 'forty miles from England'. The town fell off the prestigious and lucrative political party conference circuit due to a lack of investment in hotel and conference facilities.

By the turn of the millennium Scarborough had become a low-wage economy with a workforce ill-equipped to face the challenges of the twenty-first century. The empty holiday bed-and-breakfast accommodation was attracting hundreds of homeless people, some fresh out of prison, and pockets of poverty appeared, with one council ward being listed in the top 10 per cent most deprived in the country.

At that time Scarborough was not looking to change – it was focused on being a seaside town, and nothing more. Business yields were poor in the hospitality sector, and discounting was seen as the only option to maintain a competitive edge. However, work led by Scarborough Council was

having some positive effects, which were recognised by the Most Improved Resort Gold Award from Marketing in Tourism. European funding was also secured to help regenerate some of the town's suburban housing estates.

A major impetus came in the autumn of 2001 when Yorkshire Forward, then the Regional Development Agency for Yorkshire and Humberside, launched its Urban Renaissance programme, led by Alan Simpson. The programme, a response to Richard Rogers's 'Urban White Paper' published the previous year, had the ambition of creating a 'World Class Region', and viewed environmental quality as a driver for social and economic regeneration.

John Thompson & Partners (JTP) and West 8 from the Netherlands were appointed from the Yorkshire Forward consultant panel to create a vision for Scarborough, with an action plan for its delivery. The aim of the vision-building process was to work with the local community to explore every asset of the town and create a consensus as to how Scarborough could throw off its outdated image and move confidently into the future.

VISION
Following an initial period of research and 'community animation', which involved talking to many residents and stakeholders, the process culminated in 'Scarborough's Renaissance Community Planning Weekend'. This five-day charrette was held at the Spa Conference Centre in April 2002, with over 1,000 people taking part in two days of topic workshops and hands-on planning sessions.

The public event began with a welcome from Eileen Bosomworth, then leader of Scarborough Council, and an address by playwright Sir Alan Ayckbourn, long-term resident and director of the town's well-known Stephen Joseph Theatre. His motivational speech highlighted the rare combination of assets, both environmental and community, that existed in Scarborough, and on which the renaissance of the

View of South Bay, Scarborough, looking towards the castle

RIGHT FIGURE 5.6.2:
**Stephen Joseph Theatre
– Rounders' dramatised
interpretation of
regeneration**

BELOW FIGURE 5.6.3:
**Participants at the
Community Planning
Weekend**

town could be built. Talented members of Rounders, the Stephen Joseph Youth Theatre, dramatised life in the town and the meaning of regeneration in a highly entertaining ten-minute performance.

Teenagers, youth workers and students from several schools participated in the charrette, an open and informal event that gave people the opportunity to take part in workshops on topics such as Arts, Culture and Entertainment, Housing and Young People. The final session on the Friday focused on hands-on planning, where ideas from the workshops were discussed in more

detail, around plans of the town, plotting opportunities and starting to produce ideas for positive change. One participant said that it was a liberating process compared with typical town meetings, as the event encouraged a much more pleasant and productive dialogue.

The workshops continued on the Saturday morning, and in the afternoon participants divided into eight groups and went out into the streets to study particular parts of the town. Returning to the spa, the groups recorded their ideas on plans and presented them back to the whole assembly in a plenary session.

One unexpected outcome was that local authority officers found themselves free to discuss ideas and were empowered to introduce concepts into the process (previously they had not felt able).

Over the following three days, the twenty-seven-strong charrette team analysed and evaluated the outcomes from the two public days. The vision was presented to a large audience at the spa on the evening of Tuesday 30 April.

A number of key themes emerged, which identified important areas of consensus. These were to promote the town's strategic role in the region as a whole; to develop a quality public space strategy; to prioritise the development of flagship projects; to promote a cultural renaissance; to encourage economic development; to create strong, stable and healthy communities and to plan for growth.

Throughout the vision-building process, it was acknowledged that Scarborough is a multifaceted town and should be recognised and supported as such. Its 'ten towns in one' character defined it as a cultural town, a festival town, a heritage town, a healthy town, a tourist town, a living town, a learning town, an investment town and a 365-day 360-degree town.

The vision was neither a rigid plan nor a blueprint – it represented a new direction for the town and its people, and one that was based on shared and positive values and confirmed the need for change, for higher quality, for a new image and for a better environment.

As a first step a new Town Team, in association with several Action Teams, was established. This Town Team was given the power, together with Yorkshire Forward and the borough council, to sign off Yorkshire Forward Renaissance funding coming into Scarborough.

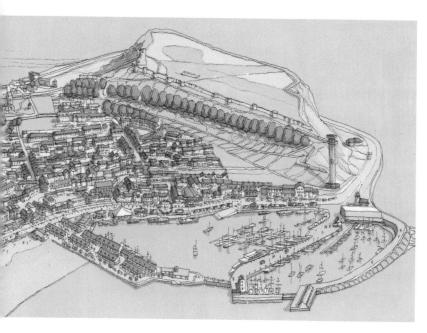

ABOVE FIGURE 5.6.5:
Aerial image of the vision for Scarborough Harbour

The extensive 'community animation' was documented in 'A Cultural Audit of Scarborough', which unveiled the potential of the creative community to help drive change. Specific arts-related improvements have since been implemented, including regeneration of the Rotunda Museum, one of the first purpose-built museums in the world, the development of Woodend Creative Workspace with over fifty studio spaces, the restoration of the Scarborough Open Air Theatre, and ongoing arts and cultural festivals. Andrew Clay, director at Woodend, believes that 'the Arts community feels secure and connected, whereas before people felt isolated – the strong legacy of the process is people being connected and feeling they can make things happen'.

Over the years following the charrette, £25m of strategic investment influenced a private sector response of more than £300m investment in the town. This has resulted in the protection or creation of more than 1,000 jobs, an improvement in business relationships and the formation of new industries.

An early focus was on the regeneration of the foreshore and harbour, described by Nick Taylor, Scarborough's Renaissance Manager, as 'the mantelpiece in the front room of the town'. Diversification of the town's economy has resulted in a £24m investment in Scarborough's business park, the construction of a new four-star hotel and an 8 per cent increase in profitability in the visitor economy.

The success of Scarborough's Renaissance has been recognised through a number of prestigious awards, all of which acknowledged the value of the participatory process: Enterprising Britain Awards First Prize (2008); European Enterprise Awards Grand Jury First Prize (2009); International Association for Public Participation's (IAP2) Project of the Year (2009); Academy of Urbanism Great Town Award (2010).

The council and the business community recently partnered to make a successful

HINDSIGHT

The Town Team drew up the 'Scarborough Renaissance Charter' in the months following the Community Planning Weekend. Town Team members were asked to help define the long-term strategy for Scarborough and clarify the objectives and action points that had been identified. They were asked to 'leave politics at the door'. An early action, aimed at changing perceptions, was the grassing of St Nicholas Street in front of the Royal Hotel, and a free open-air showing of the movie *Little Voice*, which was made in Scarborough.

A Renaissance Forum was established, meeting monthly with an attendance of between 100 and 150 people. Action Teams were formed, each focusing on a particular area of common interest and developing further key issues that had been identified at the Planning Weekend. A representative from each Action Team was nominated to join the Town Team, which thereby encompassed the interests of the Renaissance Forum as a whole. Fifteen years later, several of these groups continue to meet and discuss their areas of interest.

Scarborough University Technical College opened in 2016

competitive bid to national government to fund a new University Technical College (UTC) in Scarborough.

The UTC opened in September 2016. It is providing skills training for national and local industry, including a new multimillion pound potash mine and the expansion of Government Communications Headquarters (GCHQ), which is bringing over 1,000 new jobs to the town. Both organisations have sponsored suites at the UTC, enabling students to be job-ready on completion of

their education. David Kelly, Scarborough's Head of Economic Development, believes 'this would never have happened without the renaissance process fifteen years ago'.

URRIDAHOLT – DARING TO BE DIFFERENT
REYKJAVIK, ICELAND

DATE **NOVEMBER 2004**   CLIENT SECTOR **PRIVATE**   SITE **RURAL**
SCALE **NEIGHBOURHOOD**   VISION **PLANNING   GREEN DESIGN   URBAN DESIGN**

A new, walkable neighbourhood on the outskirts of Reykjavik was created, integrating mixed-use development with protected nature. This was the first international project to achieve final certification under the BREEAM Communities Standard 2012.

I knew what a community planning process could do, so I suggested that we should have a charrette with the town council to develop an initial vision – it can be extremely helpful when you have the whole team working towards the same goal.'

Halldora Hreggvidsdottir, Alta Consulting

FORESIGHT
Iceland is a small island nation situated in the North Atlantic just below the Arctic Circle, with a temperate tundra climate warmed by the Gulf Stream. The country's economy was severely affected by the global financial crisis in 2008, which caused a depression. The recovery of the economy has been aided by a surge in tourism, with visitors coming to enjoy the country's unique culture and its volcanic and glacial landscape.

The vast majority of the country's population of 340,000 live in Reykjavik, which

benefits from a ready supply of low-cost, renewable geothermal power. Iceland's small population has resulted in cheap land and urban sprawl, with large, low-density residential suburbs creating an over-dependence on the car.

Gardabær is a small suburban town on the outskirts of Reykjavik, which had been identified for expansion. The identified growth area included Urridaholt, a previously undeveloped hillside adjacent to the pristine Urridavatn Lake. The hill serves as a gateway from the city of Reykjavik to the natural landscape beyond. It rises around 50 m (160 ft) above a lava field, with spectacular views to the mountains, volcanoes and sea.

In 2003 the developer of Urridaholt, Jon Palmi Gudmundsson, contacted Halldora Hreggvidsdottir from Alta Consulting, Iceland to ask Alta to do a Strategic Environmental Assessment (SEA). This was intended to evaluate the potential impact of a proposed

residential and retail development at Urridaholt on the shallow Urridavatn Lake, and look at how any impacts could be mitigated.

Based on the SEA, it was decided to go ahead with the urban expansion, and Alta was asked to project manage the development of a masterplan for Urridaholt and a nearby retail development. The year before, Halldora had worked with John Thompson & Partners (JTP) to run Iceland's first ever Community Planning Weekend, and she suggested running the same type of charrette process to develop a consensus vision for the development of Urridaholt.

VISION
An initial charrette was held with council politicians and officers, and included a site visit, briefing, dialogue workshops and hands-on planning design groups. It is typical for Icelandic suburban housing developments to be built out in standard

FIGURE 5.7.1:
View of Urridaholt and Urridavatn Lake

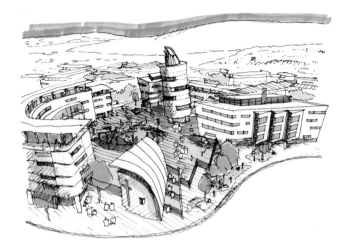

car-focused street layouts, with uniform low-density residential plots. Three days of collaborative working created a new high-level vision for a walkable, climatically responsive, mixed-use neighbourhood, with the lake and lava protected as much as possible.

Following the charrette, 'Seeing is Believing' tours were arranged to mixed-use neighbourhoods in Sweden, Denmark, Germany and the UK, and this helped

convince the council to change the municipal plan to allow a mix of uses on the site.

Three months after the initial charrette, in spring 2005, the local community were invited to a Community Planning Weekend, held in a golf club overlooking the site.

Participants were introduced to the proposed development concepts and were then invited to take part in workshops, walkabouts and hands-on planning sessions to consider challenges and opportunities for the site.

The consensus that emerged through the process was the desire to create a highly sustainable community, with calmed streets and green links to the protected lake and the wider natural environment. Following the public workshops, the consultant team drew up a vision for the site, incorporating ideas from the Winter Cities movement, which was presented back to the community at Gardebær Music Hall.

Gunnar Edmondson, current mayor of Gardebær, participated in the whole process: 'It was very enjoyable to participate and good to see the ambitious approach being taken by the developers and the professionals from the beginning to ensure quality and good placemaking. It is a model for new developments that are now being planned in Gardebær.'

HINDSIGHT
Based on the vision, a masterplan was developed that rejected suburban sprawl typologies in favour of a compact, diverse, mixed-use development. The masterplan focused on environmental and social sustainability, and was closely connected to the natural environment. It included 1,600 residential units, 90,000 m2 (970,000 sq ft) of office and retail space, an elementary school and kindergartens, and up to 65,000 m2 (700,00 sq ft) of space for civic use. Up to 9,000 people will be living and working there when it is fully occupied.

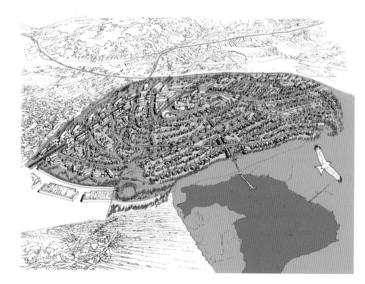

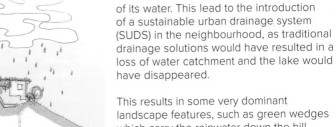

Halldora believes that the decision to create a much more sustainable development would have been impossible without a charrette process. 'Great benefits came from the charrettes – the whole council planning and environmental teams had worked together on a joint vision, and even though new ideas of change emerged, people understood and supported them.'

Participants pointed out the importance of protecting the lake and the cleanliness

of its water. This lead to the introduction of a sustainable urban drainage system (SUDS) in the neighbourhood, as traditional drainage solutions would have resulted in a loss of water catchment and the lake would have disappeared.

This results in some very dominant landscape features, such as green wedges which carry the rainwater down the hill when needed, but also serve as green corridors through the neighbourhood, with walkable paths and vegetation to support natural fauna. This is the first time that SUDS has been implemented in a whole neighbourhood in Iceland, and the consultation assisted greatly.

The masterplan was drawn up and an early development phase took place, which included IKEA, but the whole project came to a standstill due to the financial crash in 2008.

The development team submitted Urridaholt for BREEAM Communities certification – a method for measuring and evidencing the sustainability of large-scale development plans. The Urridaholt project became the first international project to achieve a final certification under BREEAM Communities 2012, and the first masterplan in Iceland to receive BREEAM Communities certification. It is a 100-hectare (250-acre) development that has achieved an interim certification. The Local Plan for the north side (Phase 2) is the first of the phases in Urridaholt to achieve a final certification, and did so with a Very Good rating.

After a five-year pause, development restarted in 2013, and Jon Palmi Gudmundsson recalls: 'When we reviewed the plan five years after the project was halted, we saw that the emphasis we put on environmental aspects and timeless principles of urban quality had stood the test of time.' Following the trauma of the financial crash, people in Iceland were looking for a more sustainable model for living.

FORMER MILL TO A SUSTAINABLE NEIGHBOURHOOD
VANCOUVER, CANADA

DATE **APRIL 2005** CLIENT SECTOR **PRIVATE** SITE **URBAN** SCALE **NEIGHBOURHOOD**
VISION **URBAN DESIGN GREEN DESIGN**

A vision for a new sustainable neighbourhood, on the site of a former sawmill on the Fraser River, involved a vocal and networked community from Vancouver, where everyone's favourite sport after hockey is town planning.

'We hear the questions and then we get to the answers, but we can't have the answers immediately. We need absolute honesty and patience with each other so we can have the most possible transparent and open discussion from all sides. We listen and we draw all the ideas and will bring them to the same level, so that the charrette leader can make a neutral presentation.'

Andrés Duany, DPZ

FORESIGHT

The Fraser River was first navigated from its source to the Pacific Ocean in 1808, and over the next 100 years it grew in importance in the lives of the settlers from Great Britain who lived along its banks. Logs were floated down the Fraser to Vancouver, and in the early twentieth century new sawmills were built to process the timber on an industrial scale.

In 1926 H. R. MacMillan founded the Canadian White Pine Mill, where massive hammerhead cranes hoisted timber to and from the river. In 1959 the White Pine Mill merged with the neighbouring Dominion Mill and, at its peak in the mid-1960s, the yard's thousands of workers milled enough timber to build 21,000 homes a year. Then came a period of decline, before the mill finally closed in 2001, with most of the equipment and buildings shipped to New Zealand.

In preparation for the site's regeneration, members of the local community were involved, with the City of Vancouver, in creating the East Fraser Lands Policy Statement. The 53-hectare (130-acre) site was seen as the last neighbourhood-sized development opportunity in the city of Vancouver, and the Policy Statement envisioned a community of around 7,000 homes with a mix of facilities, parkland and a new town centre.

The community found the early plans controversial. Concerns included traffic, schools and parks, and uncertainty about the funding of community benefits. Milt Bowling was one of several local community activists who had been working on a local park project. After hearing that Park Lane and Wesgroup were to be the developers, he was keen to meet them and find out how environmental issues were going to be addressed.

After work had begun to decontaminate the site, the developers announced that they were planning to commission a charrette to be run by Florida-based New Urbanist practice DPZ in mid-April 2005. Milt recalls: 'We had been working on the project for three or four years, and we'd never heard of a charrette before, but we thought, "Let's do it!"'

VISION

The week-long charrette process took place in a 300-person capacity tent, erected on the site. The DPZ design team occupied one part of the tent; the remainder provided space for the public workshops.

Charrette leader Andrés Duany introduced the process and explained the principles of

sustainable urbanism. He acknowledged the high quality of urban architecture in Central Vancouver, but said that the challenge was to take it to the next level in order to make the project 'deeply, structurally environmental'.

The charrette began with a series of community lectures and workshops. These focused on different topics including transportation, environment, parks and recreation, land use and architecture. At times, discussion was heated, and Milt Bowling admitted they were a community who were used to making themselves heard: 'We put Andrés on the hot seat a lot.'

Meanwhile, the design team worked away at a range of masterplan options, picking up on the discussions from the workshops and bringing in various genres and styles of urbanism.

At various points the design team's masterplans were reported back and discussed with the community.

TOP FIGURE 5.8.4:
Sketch from the charrette

CENTRE FIGURE 5.8.5:
Consented masterplan for River District

Matt Shillito, a planner with the City of Vancouver at the time, recalls: 'Duany was very good at capturing attention and getting people in the room to consider trade-offs. He would close down topics we had discussed earlier in the week to ensure forward progress was maintained.'

From Day five the design work ramped up to the final presentation on Day seven. Everyone, including Andrés, was surprised that no clear masterplan had emerged, and so five options were presented. All had in common an urban street and block pattern with a high-density town centre and a quality green space network linking to and addressing the Fraser River.

Reaction was guardedly positive after the feedback, and it was agreed that having creativity and input early in the process made a difference. The residents found it enjoyable, and one acknowledged that debate had been elevated 'above the usual nuts and bolts that we talk about'.

HINDSIGHT
Following the charrette the design concepts was developed and taken through planning by Vancouver-based James Cheng Architects. Work on site started in 2010, including the construction of the River District Centre and Neighbourhood Restaurant, which was completed in 2011, as an early focus for the new community.

At the time of writing, several residential phases to the west of the site are complete, with work on the town centre well under way to the east. The neighbourhoods are boldly high density, with residential buildings facing well-defined streets and public spaces. These have a timeless quality and create a high quality of place for the early residents to enjoy.

Referring back to Duany's challenge to create a 'project that's deeply, structurally environmental', River District has won a range of local, national and international awards for its planning and development processes. Its rainwater management plan and green space strategy will ensure the purity of water running into the Fraser River and the creation of ecological habitats. River District Energy will provide space heating and hot water throughout the neighbourhood, with the capacity to use a variety of renewables and sustainable energy sources. The entire community is on its way to attaining LEED Gold and Built Green Gold status.

Milt Bowling remembers that before the charrette took place there were people who were against anything and everything. However, as a representative of the community, he was able to encourage other people to speak calmly and make the most

of the opportunity to be involved. Although the community didn't get everything it had wanted – for example, rule changes subsequently led to a lower requirement for affordable housing – Milt was very positive about the process: 'The charrette was awesome – you can get the community to agree a vision and I would highly recommend it to any community that wants to be involved.'

ALDER HEY – THE HOSPITAL IN A PARK
LIVERPOOL, ENGLAND

DATE **SEPTEMBER 2005** CLIENT SECTOR **PUBLIC**
SITE **URBAN** SCALE **TOWN** VISION **PLANNING GREEN DESIGN ARCHITECTURE**

Originally established during the First World War as a US army camp hospital, Alder Hey grew into one of the largest children's hospitals in the Europe and a world leader in health care and research. After a century, it was time to modernise the facilities and build a new hospital. In October 2015, a radically new children's hospital building was opened, and a new chapter began in Alder Hey's history.

'Innovation came from the insights of the client body and the community – you actually have to listen and have a certain mindset to make the most of the opportunity. It's also about the endurance of the legacy – if people have a building they want, they will want to keep it and adapt it – people were absolutely up for something different and exciting: a landmark.'

Ben Zucchi, Design Director at BDP

FORESIGHT
In the early 2000s Alder Hey consultant Dr Jane Ratcliffe was inspired by a vision of a 'hospital in a park ... I had this idea that it should be something that's great fun for young people – a log cabin approach, at one with nature'. This developed into the idea of a hospital with views and access to the neighbouring Springfield Park environment, providing therapeutic benefits to patients and integrated with local neighbourhoods.

At that time, however, Liverpool City Council was keen to consider other sites to aid regeneration elsewhere in the city.

David Houghton was Alder Hey's Estates Manager. Having heard Ben Bolgar from the Prince's Foundation talk about collaborative planning at a conference, he asked Ben to formulate a process for Alder Hey.

Ben felt that their typical Sunday to Friday 'Enquiry by Design' process was not appropriate for Alder Hey. So after some discussion a step-by-step process was agreed, and the new hospital design concepts emerged through a carefully sequenced charrette process involving professional stakeholders, patients and their parents, and the wider community.

VISION
The first one-day mini-charrette involved six groups of nine people, including hospital and council representatives, to assess many site options around Liverpool.

Most were quickly rejected; six remained. The groups undertook high-level holistic

analyses of each site, followed by a more themed assessment, including looking at transport and environmental issues. Having visited and evaluated each site, Alder Hey emerged as the groups' clear preferred option.

The next stage was a three-day public charrette to agree wider parameters of the Alder Hey design, such as the precise hospital site and to solve transport problems. Initially, this generated a fraught discussion between the hospital and local residents, which focused on parking in residential streets and the loss of Springfield Park, but the charrette process enabled the issues and ideas to be worked through, discussed and sketched. The design team pointed out that, although it was valued, the existing park was not particularly attractive or well used, and that there was an opportunity to provide a better-designed and equipped park through the development process. By building the new hospital in the southeast corner of Springfield Park, and incorporating a multi-storey car park, the local parking situation could be improved. A new park would be built on the old hospital site in a later phase.

Phasing became a crucial factor in the collaborative process. This enabled the community to understand how construction and parking would be managed and how the redevelopment of the park would be planned.

Neil Coventry, Planning Officer from Liverpool City Council, felt that hand sketching at the charrette was very effective: 'The freshness of the drawings helped the community take on board the ideas. The design team didn't fancify the drawings – they were put on the wall just as they were.'

During the charrette team-working stage there was disagreement over an element of the design work, and the final public presentation had to be drastically reduced. The report back therefore focused on the essential elements of the concept that had emerged through the workshops. As Ben Bolgar explains: 'It turned out that the simplicity of the presentation was very positive, and people said, "This is fabulous – we wish people had spoken to us like this before – so simply and honestly."'

Over time, support for 'Alder Hey in the Park' grew among the public, and The Friends of Springfield Park was established to involve the community in the design and future management of the reconfigured park.

The third stage in the charrette process was organised without public involvement in order to consider the technical design of the hospital itself, with a view to submitting an outline planning application and formulating a brief for the public sector procurement process. Discussion focused on whether to design the hospital around the functional relationships within the institution, which can end up with complex bubble diagrams, as opposed to an urbanist masterplanning approach, which results in more flow and public and private spaces.

As no consensus emerged, one team was asked to design the hospital from inside out, and the other to design a masterplan 'loose fit' hospital, which it was felt led to a better vision for the park and a more futureproofed design.

Following the third charrette, the outline design parameters agreed during the workshop were developed into parameter

ABOVE FIGURES 5.9.3 & 5.9.3A:
Alternative hospital concept designs

RIGHT FIGURE 5.9.4:
Flower by Eleanor Brogan

staff, parents and children to make the brief richer and to incorporate the healing powers of nature and integration with the park into the scheme. One young boy said that he wanted the hospital to be 'curvy ad swerve' and not look like a hospital. A competition-winning drawing of a flower by then fifteen-year-old Eleanor Brogan was a particular inspiration for the final design. Eleanor went on to sit on the young people's design team and 'make vital decisions about the hospital from a patient's perspective'.

Ben Zucchi, Design Director at BDP, had to balance working with the community and designing a functioning hospital. The design concept, inspired by Eleanor Brogan's flower, was of the park integrating with the fingers of the hospital and flowing in to meet the public atrium area.

Now that the new Alder Hey Hospital is complete, the next phase of the project involves demolition of the old hospital and construction of a new residential-led

plans for the outline planning application. Once outline planning was achieved, a competitive design process was undertaken which resulted in the choice of a consortium comprising John Laing, Laing O'Rourke and Interserve, with architects BDP.

HINDSIGHT
The hospital trust was keen that the original design concepts were retained, and collaborated with BDP through further workshops to ensure this. BDP also consulted with the hospital management,

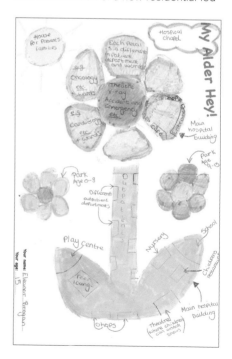

development. Unfortunately, the charrette approach was not used to formulate these proposals with the community, and they were not well received. Neil Coventry from Liverpool City Council believes they should have gone back to the community and used a workshop process, as before, to reduce the number of stumbling blocks that occurred.

The process devised by the Prince's Foundation, with Ben Bolgar acting as 'honest broker' and guiding participants through the process, ensured that crucial decisions were made in the right order with key stakeholders, turning scepticism and opposition into trust and support. The result is a new award-winning hospital, uniquely integrated into its parkland setting and providing a warm and inviting 'home from home' for young patients. Alder Hey has spacious wards with plenty of accommodation for parents, and its clinical education and research facilities are state of the art.

Dr Ratcliffe believes that the charrette processes gave an egalitarian approach to planning, but this was not random – it had form: 'Everybody can have a voice; it's not led by somebody who thinks they know best.' For Ben Bolgar the charrette approach unlocked impasses in the political process and delivered new design solutions that simply wouldn't have been possible otherwise. 'The outcome is the proof – how many modern hospitals do you know with nearly all of the windows opening on to parks and gardens?'

Dr Ratcliffe's vision of 'having nature come right into the hospital' has been realised.

A COLLAGE OF BUILDINGS ON THE RIVER THAMES

KEW BRIDGE, LONDON, ENGLAND

DATE **JULY 2006**   CLIENT SECTOR **PRIVATE**   SITE **URBAN**   SCALE **NEIGHBOURHOOD**
VISION **URBAN DESIGN ARCHITECTURE**

The Kew Bridge site was always going to be a challenge to regenerate, being a key gateway to the London Borough of Hounslow, located in a conservation area on the banks of the River Thames, lying adjacent to the Grade II* listed Kew Bridge, near Kew Steam Museum's 60 m (200 ft) high Grade I listed Italianate standpipe tower, and opposite the Kew Gardens World Heritage Site.

'There are usually a lot of dilemmas in the design process, but the collaborative process enabled consensus to be arrived at.'
John Thompson, Founder Chairman, JTP

FORESIGHT

The 0.7-hectare (1.7-acre) site had lain empty since Kew Bridge House office block and Horseferry Rowing Club were demolished in the late 1980s and early 1990s, leaving just the Waggon and Horses pub standing. In an effort to progress the redevelopment of this important site, Hounslow Council drew up and adopted a Planning and Urban Design Brief in September 2001. Their preference was for a mixed-use development for business and community uses, or mixed business and residential uses.

Developer St George West London acquired the site in 2002 and drew up a scheme that was submitted for planning consent. Council officers recommended the proposal for approval, but fierce objections from the local community led to it being refused at planning committee stage. The application was then dismissed at appeal, although the planning inspector gave helpful guidance for any future proposals, including the importance of retaining views to the Grade I listed Italianate tower, and sight lines to steps up to Kew Bridge.

Following this dismissal, St George wanted to take a fresh approach to the site and rebuild relationships with the local community. John Thompson & Partners (JTP) were appointed to draw up new proposals, through a community planning approach.

John Thompson says: 'The local community had run a successful campaign – it was probably the best-organised and most-qualified community we had ever met. We put a lot of energy into making the design process open and accessible, because

OPPOSITE FIGURE 5.10.1:
Aerial view of the vacant Kew Bridge House site

ABOVE FIGURE 5.10.2:
Hands-on planning report back

although the community were fine-tuned to object, they also realised that something was needed on the site.'

VISION

The collaborative process began with meetings with local groups from Brentford and neighbouring Strand on the Green to introduce the new design team and find out more about community concerns and aspirations. In parallel, workshops were arranged with children from local schools, and meetings were held with the local authority and other statutory organisations.

The 'Kew Bridge Community Planning Weekend' began with a briefing and an area tour for the facilitation team members. Around 100 people attended the two public workshops that took place on a Friday and Saturday in July 2006. A key focus of the public sessions was a thorough explanation of the planning brief requirements, and the additional guidance given by the inspector's report. With this in mind, participants debated the issues and developed ideas for the site and its relationship with the surrounding area.

Local resident Peter Browne recalls: 'The event was held very professionally – the lead facilitator was saying, "This is what we are here for, this is what we are trying to do." It channelled people's input to what they could influence.'

Key themes to emerge included respecting site context and views, architectural design, height and massing, physical connections and sustainability. Another particular focus was on the need for public space by the riverside, as there was a lack of public access to the water.

Important design principles included the need for the site to be opened up visually and physically, with through routes from Strand on the Green, and a landscaped public space. It was suggested that the building design could have a stepped form down to the river, and instead of

one single building, there should be a collection of smaller buildings at a human scale. The building line should be set back from Kew Bridge Road, with the highest part of the scheme towards the centre or near the neighbouring Thameside Centre development, away from Kew Bridge.

Malcolm Wood, former Land Director for St George, thinks there were several key benefits to holding a Community Planning Weekend. This included the opportunity to spend longer with local people. Walking around the area together helped the design team to develop relationships and understand local concerns.

Breaking into hands-on planning design groups enabled people to recognise the complexities of developing a site, as well as giving them a voice.

Following the public workshops, the charrette team drew up an illustrated vision, which was presented back to the community the following Thursday evening, Day seven of the Community Planning Weekend process. The vision included a development designed as 'a collage of buildings' with homes and ground floor commercial and community uses set around a public piazza next to the river. Importantly, the feedback also explained why certain ideas discussed during the workshops could not be incorporated.

Malcolm Wood was very positive about the approach followed by JTP: 'A weakness of this sort of process can be raising people's expectations, but this was handled well at Kew Bridge, where we were clear and transparent about the parameters.'

With the report back taking place so quickly after the event, people could easily recall their involvement in the public workshops. They could see that they had been carefully listened to and that their ideas had been given proper consideration. The design approach was explained in depth. A key aspect was the creation of a large portion of public realm that was accessible to all.

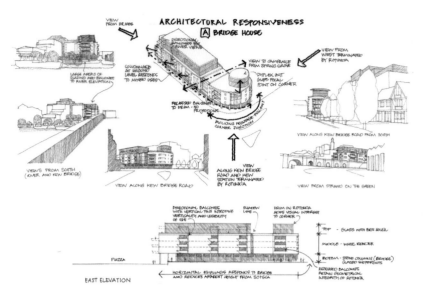

ARCHITECTURAL RESPONSIVENESS
A BRIDGE HOUSE

EAST ELEVATION

TOP LEFT FIGURE 5.10.3:
Explanatory scheme concept drawings

TOP RIGHT FIGURE 5.10.4:
Model of the evolving scheme

CENTRE FIGURE 5.10.5:
Vignette with view through to Italianate water tower

There was a strong desire from local people to continue to be involved during the design development phase. As a result, regular design update meetings were held with St George and JTP, explaining the development of the proposals by using PowerPoint presentation and a three-dimensional model, which was reprinted between meetings to show the design changes.

HINDSIGHT

Following a pre-submission exhibition, a detailed planning application for Kew Bridge was submitted in 2009, which was granted the following year. The new proposals differed significantly from the original, dismissed, scheme and included the protection of views identified by the inspector, a more responsive frontage to the river, and an increase in the setback from Kew Bridge Road. The final design focused on creating a new destination, which included a riverside piazza and an improved riverside walkway with a south-facing aspect over the Thames towards Kew Gardens.

St George subsequently acquired the Waggon and Horses pub, as well as the neighbouring Thameside Centre offices. This extended the Kew Bridge site, and the additional area was incorporated into a new masterplan, which was granted planning approval in 2011.

The development, completed in 2016, comprises a range of mixed uses including a new riverside pub, restaurants, shops, offices, a boating club and 308 new homes (149 more than the initial permission). The scheme opened up views to the river from

Kew Bridge Road (an original aspiration from the Community Planning Weekend) and just over 50 per cent of the site area is publicly accessible open space. New trees and green spaces have created a high-quality landscaped environment, including a riverside walk.

The result is a unique development that has enhanced its riverside location and created a new destination. John Thompson believes that Kew Bridge is one of the best examples of a well-designed ongoing collaborative design process, as people were made aware of the inevitable compromises that had to be made.

Peter Browne, a local resident, describes how the collaborative process was a positive experience and achieved practical results that enhanced the local area in a way that the community wanted: 'The community pushed for a different architectural style and layout, and this was taken on board. It has also enabled the people to use the public areas by the river, which were never used before. I have no doubt these community workshop processes are successful, and I have to say we could hold this one up as the gold standard.'

RESTITCHING A UNESCO WORLD HERITAGE CITY
LÜBECK ALTSTADT, GERMANY

DATE **MARCH 2007** CLIENT SECTOR **PUBLIC/THIRD** SITE **URBAN** SCALE **CITY** VISION **URBAN DESIGN**

The 'Mitten in Lübeck' charrette stimulated more than 400 local people to contribute to the design of the public realm to restitch the historic fabric of a UNESCO World Heritage City.

'What was special was the broad participation of the population and the interdisciplinary discussion – and the way the working groups resolved issues together.'

Hans-Walter Rechter, cycling officer for Lübeck

ABOVE FIGURE 5.11.1:
Aerial photo of Lübeck

FORESIGHT

Lübeck is a historic Hanseatic League City near Hamburg in northern Germany. The old quarter, identified by UNESCO as a World Heritage Site, is an island enclosed by the Trave River and the Elbe-Lübeck Canal, with a medieval plan reflecting the function of the island during its heyday as a port. Königstrasse, the central north–south street, is like a backbone with 'ribs' running down to the waterfront on either side. Goods were conveyed to and fro along the ribs to the magnificent merchants' houses built along the central axis.

The city consisted of seven neighbourhoods, each represented by its own church, and Lübeck is also known for being home to Thomas Mann at the time he wrote the novel *Buddenbrooks* (1901).

The old quarter suffered damage from Allied bombs during the Second World War, and postwar reconstruction was functional but uninspiring in contrast to the grandeur, beauty and materiality of the traditional buildings and streets. The city centre also went through a phase of being dominated by vehicle traffic, until key streets were pedestrianised in the 1980s and 1990s.

Today Lübeck has grown to a population of over 200,000, and the island itself remains the commercial and cultural heart. It is a major tourist attraction but also a living and working place, with retail facilities serving local people alongside shops and restaurants for visitors.

By the early 2000s the city authorities had decided that they wanted to invest in the quality of the public realm, in part due to Lübeck's UNESCO status. The funding was to be provided in large part by the Possehl Foundation, influential city guardians working to preserve the city's beauty, among other things. However, the stakeholders could not agree on a course of action, and it was decided to throw the process open to the wider community in an attempt to create a consensus plan.

VISION

In 2006 Von Zadow International (VZI) and John Thompson & Partners (JTP), were commissioned to carry out a *Perspektivenwerkstatt* (charrette), with Gehl Architects from Copenhagen forming part of the team. The first step of the process was the establishment of a steering group backed by a wider *Unterstützerkreis* (support circle) with around thirty members from the Lübeck community. The support circle has been a favoured approach in other community planning processes in Germany, as it engages a wide network directly in the organisation of the charrette. The resulting benefits include representatives becoming better acquainted with the process, spreading the word to their networks, helping to publicise the charrette widely,

and ensuring better and more informed participation, leading to more involvement in the organisation of the event.

VZI facilitated regular steering group and support circle meetings over several months to organise logistics (including recruiting a bilingual local team to help run the public workshops) and publicity in the run-up to the 'Mitten in Lübeck Perspektivenwerkstatt', which was held in March 2007.

The charrette spanned seven days, beginning on a Thursday with a team briefing and site visit. On the Friday and Saturday the community were invited to participate in dialogue workshops, hands-on planning groups and walkabouts. In particular, groups considered the quality of existing streets and public spaces, bearing in mind a quality scoring methodology devised with Gehl Architects.

Hans-Walter Rechter, the cycling officer for Lübeck at the time of the charrette, recalls: 'What was special was the broad participation of the population, and the interdisciplinary discussion, and the way the working groups resolved issues together.' Another event participant commented: 'It's

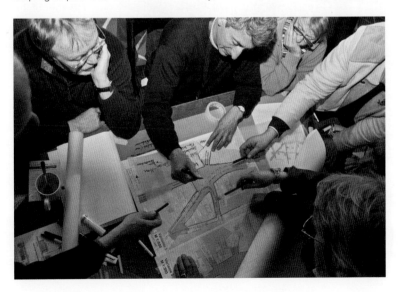

RIGHT FIGURE 5.11.2: **'Delta' workshop considering design options for a key space in Lübeck**

surprising how much agreement there is between everyone – usually when we come together we just discuss controversies.'

The JTP team worked for four days from the Sunday morning to develop the vision for the city centre, which was presented back to the community on the Wednesday evening. The design concept built on the heritage of the city's structure, including public realm and lighting proposals. These were based on the characterisation of different public spaces as, for example, 'artistic', 'tranquil', 'arrival', 'see and be seen', 'high quality market square', 'history', and so on. Following on from work done by the hands-on planning

groups, the design team undertook a 'before and after' evaluation of key public spaces. This assessed how the proposals would improve the spaces in terms of different aspects of quality.

One hands-on planning group, called 'Delta', had looked in detail at the circulation of traffic around the city. As a result, it was proposed to close Schmiedestrasse to enable the transformation of Klingenberg – a key space – into a lively public square. Part of the appeal of this idea was that participants recalled how much they had enjoyed using public spaces during the 2006 Football World Cup, hosted by Germany, when large screens were erected to show the matches in cities all over the country.

The closure of the Schmiedestrasse was a possible measure that the local authority's traffic department had been aware for decades, but that they had been hesitant to bring forward for fear of opposition from the local community. The open and collaborative atmosphere of the charrette created the conditions for the decision to be agreed – literally within a few minutes – assisted by the fact that the reporting back of this idea was done by local residents rather than a member of the professional team.

While the focus of the initiative was on upgrading the public realm, an opportunity was identified for a new building to be created on an underused, linear pedestrianised space called Schrangen. A proposal emerged for a pavilion building containing a cafe with a roof terrace that would work as a viewing space on to activities in the square, with the cathedral as a magnificent backdrop.

The vision received enthusiastic public and institutional support, and went on to form the brief for an international design competition. At the report back Bausenator Franz-Peter Boden, Councillor for Urban Planning, declared: 'If all future community planning events in Lübeck are as competent and creative, I do not fear about Lübeck's future.'

BELOW FIGURE 5.11.4:
**New water feature in a
pedestrianised street**

HINDSIGHT

Following the Community Planning Weekend the city authorities arranged an international competition to carry out the visionary proposals. Fred London from JTP and a local charrette team member were invited on to the jury to maintain the continuity of the process and the concepts behind the design. A local practice won the competition, and many of the proposals have now been implemented, including the closure of the Schmiedestrasse and the creation of a new public space on the Klingenberg. The Lübeck community and visitors now enjoy beautifully designed pedestrian areas – several with water features – in an animated and people-focused city centre. The public realm improvements enhance the historic built environment of this important World Heritage destination.

Hans-Walter Rechter concludes: 'The workshops prepared the way for renewal of the Lübeck pedestrian zone, and today you can see the results daily. In particular, the reconfiguration of the Klingenberg would have been impossible to agree without the charrette.'

BELOW FIGURE 5.11.4:
**New water feature in a
pedestrianised street**

AN AREA PLAN FOR THE HOME OF GUINNESS
DUBLIN, IRELAND

DATE **NOVEMBER 2007**   CLIENT SECTOR **PUBLIC**   SITE **URBAN**   SCALE **NEIGHBOURHOOD**
VISION **PLANNING   URBAN DESIGN**

In 2007 Dublin was booming, and The Liberties, home of the Guinness Brewery since 1759, was in need of public sector investment and simultaneously facing huge pressure from private sector developers. Dublin City Council decided to work with the local community to draw up a Development Framework Plan – the aim being to regenerate The Liberties as a more exciting, attractive and liveable city quarter.

'Diageo couldn't ignore the process and I think the fact that we focused on Guinness land brought to bear a lot of reflection on what they should do with it. I do think the process may have influenced Diageo, who finally decided not to leave the area.'

Evelyn Hanlon, Project Manager, Dublin City Council

FORESIGHT
The Liberties is located directly southwest of the walls of Viking and medieval Dublin. Due to its location on the Liffey and Poddle rivers and at the junction of important routes from each corner of Ireland, it became a major industrial centre, and textiles led the way.

Following the decline of the textiles industry in the late eighteenth century, the brewing industry took over as a major employer. In 1759, Arthur Guinness leased a 1.6-hectare (4-acre) site at £45 per year for 9,000 years. Guinness was to become the largest brewery in Ireland in 1838, and by the beginning of the twentieth century the largest in the world.

From 1961 to 1991, a declining Dublin lost half of its population and saw high levels of deprivation in the city, including in The Liberties. But the rapid economic growth during the 'Celtic Tiger' period meant that by the turn of the twenty-first century the city's fortunes had reversed. The population of The Liberties grew by 66 per cent over fifteen years, with an increasingly diverse community. The resulting patchwork of highly affluent and highly deprived neighbourhoods became one of the defining characteristics of the area.

By 2007 The Liberties was facing significant development pressure and major change. Improvements to Dublin's public transport infrastructure were planned which would significantly improve the connectivity of the area, and a number of large brownfield sites were becoming available for redevelopment. In addition, the Dublin City Council (DCC) housing in the area needed investment and renewal.

Another issue of concern was a confirmation by Guinness owner Diageo that it was considering moving the 250-year-old brewery out of The Liberties.

In 2007, DCC appointed John Thompson & Partners (JTP) with Metropolitan Workshop and John Spain Associates to draw up a Regeneration Framework Plan and to guide future investment and strike a balance between protecting the heritage of the historic city quarter. It would take into consideration the needs of the local residential and commercial community, and promote new development that would enable The Liberties to become a more exciting, attractive and liveable city quarter.

VISION
A key element of developing the strategy was to engage with the community. Following a series of initial neighbourhood workshops held in the Pimlico, Liberties and Grand Canal/Basin Lane areas in early October, the 'New Vision for The Liberties Community Planning Weekend' ran from Thursday 8 to Wednesday 14 November 2007.

The charrette began with a local traders' workshop on the Thursday evening. Day two took place at St Catherine's Church and started with a team briefing and tour of The Liberties area. The first session of public workshops commenced with a brief introduction and report back from a local school children's workshop. Participants then took part in workshops and hands-on planning groups, discussing issues and ideas and recording their suggestions on plans. In addition, a team went out to the Meath Street Market to engage with people in the street.

On Day three the venue changed to the Digital Hub in Crane Street, close to the Guinness Brewery, and concentrated on hands-on planning activities. Walkabout groups focused on different parts of the study area and returned to the venue to draw up ideas, before presenting them to the whole group in a plenary session.

Evelyn Hanlon, the city council's project manager, remembers the importance of choosing different types of venues – places that were familiar to local people.

Following the public workshops, the team worked for four days to draw up a 'Vision for The Liberties', which was reported back to the community on the Wednesday evening as a PowerPoint presentation and summary newsletter.

A number of key themes were identified. These focused on building trust and managing the process of change to improve the image of the area and bring benefits to the existing community, while ensuring integration with incoming people. New developments should complement, not threaten, the heritage of the area, and careful urban design should integrate old and new in a high-quality, safe and walkable urban environment.

Encouraging tourism and supporting the creative, digital economy was to be an important part of developing a vibrant,

A key outcome of the collaborative process was the formation of The Liberties Public Forum and five focus groups, which met monthly for almost a year. Emerging proposals were regularly presented to the forum and amended in response to comments received. Facilitated by consultants, the focus groups developed action plans, which focused on Built Heritage & the Thomas Street ACA; Environmental Sustainability; Arts & Culture; Sports Leisure & Recreation and Biodiversity & Open Space.

HINDSIGHT

One characteristic of the process in The Liberties was the length of time it took to involve certain groups of people. The continuity of community engagement following the Planning Weekend was key to the successful connection with groups such as the community who ran the horse-drawn tours from the brewery. After some months they too started to come to the public events and contribute their concerns and ideas.

After the initial stages of the community planning process, DCC held meetings with landowners. This resulted in land to the north of Thomas Street and up to the River Liffey being included in the redevelopment area.

It was also agreed to upgrade the strategy to the production of a full Liberties Area Plan (LAP). The parameters for regeneration – and thus consultation – were widened, and a series of area meetings were held to include local people and stakeholders from the extended study areas in the process, which in turn further informed the LAP. Evelyn Hanlon considers that the process helped define The Liberties: 'People wanted to be inside the boundary, so it was extended. There was a coming together of the people to be part of a recognised brand of The Liberties.'

At the time of the LAP process, Diageo, owner of Guinness, was talking about leaving Dublin. Evelyn feels that the engagement process was a key factor in

modern city quarter while also providing the community and educational amenities for a thriving residential population.

The vision created three main character neighbourhoods to help give a mental map of The Liberties area and strengthen connections:

• **The Creative Core** – centred around Thomas Street and linking the theatres of the east to the Digital Hub in the centre and on to the Guinness land and St James Harbour to the west via a new tourist trail.

• **The Quays** – busy roads and industry dominated the river frontages in this area, which were reconfigured into a rich mixed-use format celebrating the Liffey and transforming its banks into a new series of interconnected public open spaces.

• **The Markets** – Meath and Francis streets were joined by a redeveloped Newmarket to create a 'market loop' southwards off the Creative Core, and supported by the Vicar Street artisans' area and the indoor Iveagh Markets to the north.

BELOW FIGURE 5.12.4:
**Aerial drawing of the
vision for The Liberties**

Diageo deciding to remain in The Liberties. In 2012 Guinness announced a further €150m investment in the site.

To enable people to better understand the proposals, a model of the area was commissioned by City Architect Ali Grehan. The making of a physical model was well worth the cost – it showed that the scale of proposals was appropriate, and not threatening. As a result, many concerns simply evaporated.

At the time of writing The Liberties is undergoing a renaissance, with almost €1 billion of public and private sector investment in housing, commercial and tourism planned for the area. The Liberties Business Area Improvement Initiative has been set up to coordinate DCC and private sector investment in the physical environment, to promote cultural life and activities, and, together with its partners in The Liberties Business Forum, to promote and market The Liberties.

This new confidence in and the desire to be associated with the area is well illustrated by the announcement in 2017 of a new €25m Irish whiskey distillery to be built by Diageo. In a press statement, Operations Director Colin O'Brien said: 'The investment further demonstrates Diageo's commitment to the growing vibrancy of The Liberties, one of the city's most dynamic districts.'

REVITALISING THE TOWN THAT ROOFED THE WORLD

BLAENAU FFESTINIOG, GWYNEDD, WALES

DATE **OCTOBER 2008**   CLIENT SECTOR **PUBLIC/THIRD**   SITE **URBAN**
SCALE **TOWN**   VISION **URBAN DESIGN**

Around Blaenau Ffestiniog they say that 'the mountains have been turned inside out'. Approaching the town by rail through the verdant beauty of the Snowdonia National Park, the traveller's experience is instantly transformed as the train passes through a gateway of huge slate-grey heaps of blasted rock, the vestiges of over two centuries of slate quarrying. The decline of the industry had a severe economic and social impact on the town, and a group of locals set about reviving its fortunes.

'The artist comes with his or her own vocabulary. This is combined with the ideas from members of the community and the inspiration of the place and its distinctiveness. A key part of the collaboration is our professional input. We are professional designers and there comes a point when you simply have to design.'

Howard Bowcott, Artist

FORESIGHT

Blaenau owes its origins to the slate industry. The town was predominantly built in the 1860s as a result of a phenomenal boom in production, when slate was sent all over the world. At its peak in the 1870s the town 'that roofed the world' was the second largest in Wales, with over 11,000 inhabitants. Then came decline, as cheaper imports from Spain and mass-produced clay tiles undermined the competitiveness of the Blaenau quarries.

Today, the population is at less than half its peak, and the long decline of the slate industry has inevitably placed economic and social strains on the town. However, the remaining residents have a profound sense of community and a deep connection with the unique heritage and culture that grew out of the slate industry.

By the early twenty-first century, Blaenau was at a tipping point. While there was low business confidence and a poor town centre offer, with a third of high street shops empty, there was also a huge opportunity for the town to capitalise on the burgeoning visitor economy in the area.

The boundaries of Snowdonia National Park exclude Blaenau itself, but its setting puts the town at the centre of the iconic region. Residents insist that 'It's not the hole, it's the heart.' The heritage railway was a key attractor, but on arrival at the station passengers were faced with a blank retaining wall blocking the view to the town centre. There was little visible to entice visitors to stop.

OPPOSITE FIGURE 5.13.1:
View of Blaenau Ffestiniog with slate spoil in the foreground

ABOVE FIGURE 5.13.2:
Stakeholders about to board the train at Tan-y-Bwlch station

The local community began to debate the need for a regeneration strategy, while at the same time the Ffestiniog Railway Company was considering what improvements could be made to the station area.

An initial brainstorming day was convened by the community, in partnership with Gwynedd Council, to consider the issues and opportunities and come up with ideas for launching a new regeneration strategy. The council agreed to provide funding for a feasibility study and design development, in the knowledge that European Regional Development Funds were available to bid for if the right projects emerged.

The regeneration project began in 2007 as a partnership between Gwynedd Council, the local community group Blaenau Ymlaen (Blaenau Forward) and the Welsh Government. Miller Research was appointed as lead consultant with regeneration specialist Chris Jones as project manager. Community engagement was to be paramount, with representatives from Blaenau Ymlaen on the project team from the outset to help steer the process.

Major physical interventions were considered essential, the retail offer was to be improved, and tourism was to be invested in, celebrating the unique aspects of the town's heritage, culture and setting. The aim was to implement an innovative design and planning strategy that showcased Blaenau Ffestiniog's remarkable heritage, while looking to the future and proclaiming that the town was open for business.

VISION

The community involvement needed to be genuine and highly relevant to the place and local culture. An innovative charrette process was devised to maximise engagement and maintain the required pace of the programme. A requirement was bilingual communication through the use of the Welsh and English languages. In addition, artist Howard Bowcott was part of the team engaged to work with the community.

The first stakeholder workshop started at Tan-y-Bwlch station on the Ffestiniog Railway, some thirty minutes' steam train ride from the town centre. As Chris Jones explains, in what is a metaphor for the whole process: 'We took people on a journey.'

Before boarding the train, participants were divided into role-play groups of town centre users, such as local shoppers, a retired couple, a young family, investors and a young professional couple. People were asked: 'What do you want to find when you arrive?'

Groups worked in the train carriage, discussing their thoughts and ideas. On arrival in Blaenau they explored the town, having been asked the questions 'Does the town deliver what you want?' and 'What is missing and what could be improved?' All of the groups then reconvened to feed back their experiences and to discuss and draw up their future aspirations for the town

centre. Instead of the ubiquitous sticky notes, Blaenau roofing slates were used, on which participants chalked up ideas and created a slate wall gallery of words for future action.

A wider community event followed the stakeholder session, during which local people were asked about their town centre by means of an 'issues and opportunities' mapping session, led by design team members. The use of slate tiles continued with the creation of an extensive list of visionary statements, in addition to some action points. This process attracted the direct participation of over 150 local residents plus online contributions.

Following these two workshop days the design team drew up a vision for the town incorporating art in the public realm, with focus on the town's gateways and the central area around the railway station. The proposed artworks, including four iconic slate pillars by the station, were inspired by the cultural heritage of the town. The vision was reported back first to the Blaenau Ymlaen board and then to the wider community.

The design philosophy of the vision built on Blaenau's heritage, culture and location and looked to the future with confidence.

The slate tips and quarry railways became important reference points, with quarry inclines determining the key axis to the overall design.

Outdoor tourism was identified as a key growth area, and the design and planning team worked closely with the Antur Stiniog downhill mountain bike trails, the green town initiative and walking and cycling activities. The philosophy informing the planning process was to provide the 'glue' that connected the various initiatives.

On adoption of the vision, the team took the initial concept through to options development. Both Chris Jones and Howard Bowcott saw the retention of the consultant team as key to the integrity of the project and the continuity of a strong working relationship with the local community.

An options development workshop for stakeholders and a public exhibition held in December 2008 helped local people and stakeholder organisations consider the choices and determine their main priorities.

Slate pillars took the place of the retaining wall, their shape inspired by a slate chisel given to Howard by a member of the community. A further key element of the

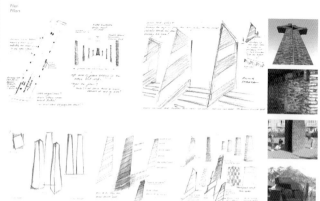

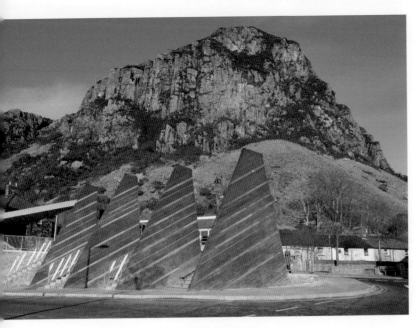

ABOVE FIGURE 5.13.6:
The pillars installed

celebrating the town's unique heritage while building community pride and confidence and creating a natural stopping point for visitors, thereby encouraging spending in the town centre.

Innovative, collaborative placemaking and investment helped revive a town centre previously stuck in a spiral of decline. At the time of writing, retail unit vacancy rates are at just 10 per cent, markedly down from 2007 levels. This has happened through a period of post-credit-crunch austerity, and despite some missed opportunities to further consolidate footfall in the town centre, such as the failure to extend the final stage of the Antur Stiniog downhill mountain biking trail to end in the town centre.

Reflecting on the impact of the project, Chris Jones considers that the process, which was started by the community, has raised aspirations and led to a significant economic upturn. The scheme increased social cohesion and confidence in Blaenau, which is now well placed to build on the progress of the last few years.

To a large extent, it is now up to the residential and business community to exploit the opportunity created by the investment, to continue to develop the services and hospitality in the town, to attract and retain visitors, and sustain a vibrant economy.

Eifion Williams, a member of the Blaenau Ymlaen, sadly passed away in early 2017, but his comment underlines the importance of the process: 'It has made North Wales the centre of activity – Blaenau started it off – the whole area has gained. We need now to take full advantage.'

design was the 'Votty axis', a straight slate transportation line down the hill to the town, which by consensus became the design driver and influenced the orientation of the pillars. Height was important for the pillars, and it was crucial for the community that they framed the space but were also oriented so that the view up the Votty axis was opened up.

The project received support from over 90 per cent of the community and proceeded smoothly through planning. The planning committee meeting held in July 2009 was notable for the comments from members giving support and endorsement to the design, and community engagement as exemplars of best practice.

HINDSIGHT
The result of the process is high-quality public realm that connects key entry points, marked by the landmark slate pillars, to a revitalised town centre, and the slate heritage of the Votty axis. Imaginative use of contemporary art and design has been integrated throughout the scheme,

REGENERATING A HISTORIC WAREHOUSE PRECINCT
DUNEDIN, NEW ZEALAND

DATE **JUNE 2011**   CLIENT SECTOR **PUBLIC**   SITE **URBAN**   SCALE **NEIGHBOURHOOD**   VISION **URBAN DESIGN**

As a consequence of new earthquake-strengthening legislation, a fledgling initiative to save a unique built heritage became a comprehensive consensus-led strategy with endorsement from the city council. This resulted in the delivery of a thriving urban creative quarter, with new jobs, new residents and heritage buildings that were saved and refurbished.

'We have a group of strong and inspiring developers and the charrette really got them together. Today the building stock is world-class and there is now a definite sense of excitement and pride on the streets. We need to involve the community more to make more things happen.'

Veronica Eastell, local worker

FORESIGHT

Dunedin, the Gaelic name for Edinburgh, is a city of around 120,000 residents, situated in Otago, New Zealand's South Island. One of New Zealand's oldest cities, it contains the country's first university and has many historic buildings. In recent years economic and population growth have stagnated, and the city council fell into debt. Adding to the challenges was evidence that the local community were divided in their views about what should be done.

Dave Cull, a new mayor with a strong leadership style, was determined to arrest

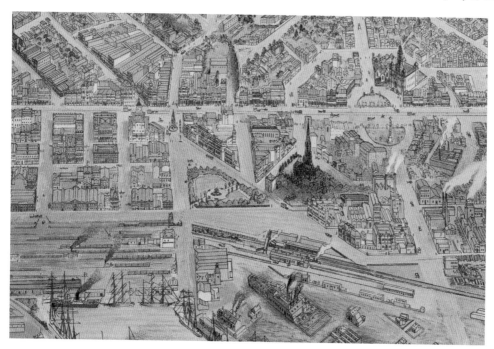

LEFT FIGURE 5.14.1:
3D map of the warehouse district from the 1890s

the stagnation and give new direction to the city. The Dunedin Central City Strategy was initiated under the leadership of City Development Manager Dr Anna Johnson and her colleague Dr Glen Hazelton. Glen had already saved some of the historic buildings in the city's virtually abandoned Warehouse Precinct. The precinct was blighted due to zoning for big-box retail development and threatened with demolition due to the costs of newly introduced earthquake-strengthening requirements.

In 2013 the council launched a regeneration initiative to create a coherent vision and the strategic initiatives required to achieve it. Key to this was gaining the confidence and support of the business sector and the wider community, identifying opportunities to boost prosperity and employment, and defining and countering risks that could weaken retail viability and diminish the character of built form and open space.

To meet the challenges and deliver the objectives a collaborative charrette-based approach seemed the logical way

forward, to integrate specialist knowledge with stakeholders' views. Consultants Urbanismplus, led by Kobus Mentz, were appointed, with a team of sub-consultants.

VISION

A substantial programme of events preceded the Dunedin Warehouse Precinct 'Enquiry by Design' (EBD) charrette, including public information communications, councillor sessions, focus group sessions and a public visioning workshop with about 100 participants. Ideas, aspirations and concerns were harvested, collated and fed back into the charrette process.

A four-day intensive technical charrette used a 'one team' approach, with consultants paired with council technical officers. This enabled high-quality expertise to be combined with local knowledge and realism. The process resulted in good follow-through due to the 'ownership' of those tasked with implementing the strategies.

Confidence was built by first listening to the views and aspirations of stakeholders,

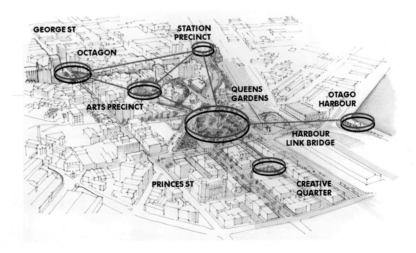

RIGHT FIGURE 5.14.2:
Concept diagram for open space and event network

BELOW LEFT FIGURE 5.14.3:
**Vignette of the
revitalised Vogel Street**

BELOW RIGHT FIGURE 5.14.4:
**Refurbished buildings
on Vogel Street**

by undertaking to investigate them, then explaining what the investigations delivered and providing a strongly justified strategy. Even where outcomes were contrary to expectations, they were accepted because the initial suggestions had been taken seriously, and people felt they had been listened to.

The final outcome included a strategy for movement, mixed uses, heritage, open space, employment, community and measures to strengthen the retail vitality and the arts precinct, and a public space upgrade of the Octagon, Dunedin's signature central public open space.

A set of public space, regulatory, procedural and financial changes were proposed with the aim of generating high-value employment in this area. Far-reaching traffic changes were proposed. These included returning to two-way the one-way pair of state highways running through the city centre, to

reconnect the heart of the city centre with the historically significant Queens Gardens and the Warehouse Precinct.

In addition, improved pedestrian connectivity between the city centre and the harbour was proposed for the long term. It was also recommended that visitor, student and night-time experiences should be developed, with a programme of events associated with the various public spaces in the city centre.

A key moment in the collaborative process was the enthusiastic buy-in from a previously divided public at the final project presentation, which emboldened elected members to give their full endorsement.

HINDSIGHT
The Dunedin Central City Strategy has been regarded a significant success, with many of its initiatives implemented. It offers a framework for future work, which will evolve as circumstances change. Initial

city council funding of NZ$500,000 was invested in public-realm improvements and further incentive funding for a building reuse grants scheme. Changes to the District Plan (the legislation controlling the land use and development) that encouraged redevelopment of historic buildings in the Warehouse Precinct were implemented, and the first $5m private sector anchor project proceeded there, resulting in new jobs.

Most notable has been the dramatic revitalisation of the Warehouse Precinct. With the public realm upgrade substantially complete, and funding and rule changes in place, the market has responded strongly.

Numerous buildings dating back as far as 1888, some vacant for up to ten years, have been saved and reoccupied through a reuse grants scheme for earthquake-strengthening and facade improvements.

Many new businesses, some of which are entirely new to Dunedin, now occupy refurbished buildings, including a new hotel in the formerly vacant historic post office. There are also several new apartment complexes, a pop-up theatre and pop-up urban winery, a microbrewery, a chocolate maker, artist studios and several cafes and coffee bars.

An analysis of the return on investment showed that for a $1.1m council investment in grants and amenity upgrades, the city has levered in $52m of private investment. With the uplifted amenity of the area the property market has shifted, and now values the heritage buildings highly as both office and residential spaces. Once-derelict heritage buildings now offer high quality and high commercial returns. Tourism opportunities have increased, and the district as a whole is providing a high-profile opportunity to market the city.

Prior to the EBD workshop, Dunedin City Council had suffered, like many other local authorities, from a silo-based approach to working. The charrette process enabled, for the first time, many departments to

work together in a focused and intense way on how to create a vibrant city centre, with a connected and repurposed Warehouse Precinct. It also provided a forum for interaction between councillors, the community and staff that put everyone on an equal footing in a spirit of genuine collaboration to identify one vision for the centre of the city, and actions across the public–private spectrum to help achieve that vision. An unanticipated consequence of the process has been that Dunedin City Council's public satisfaction ratings have improved, partly because of the implementation of this strategy. In a mid-2016 survey, residents' ratings were up by six points (to 87 per cent) from the previous year for how Dunedin maintains and preserves its architectural heritage, up seven points (to 76 per cent) on how they see Dunedin as a creative city, and up thirteen points (to 48 per cent) on being satisfied or very satisfied that the city council delivers overall value for money.

Mayor Cull described the strategy as 'an inspirational vision and incisive strategic plan that illustrates urban design's relevance in these challenging times'. It has arrested the decay in an important part of the city, rescued buildings that attest to the city's history and identity, and stimulated investment. Public trust has, to a considerable extent, been restored.

The precinct is now transformed, and the new community is looking for ways to get more involved in the next stage. Local worker and resident Veronica Eastell is very keen to continue with a participative approach to take things forward: 'I'd love the charrette process to happen again – we are in the next phase of development, and more street life is what we now need the most. We have one street festival per year but we need to involve the community to make more things happen.' This is a valuable testament to the success of the whole collaborative process, and the energy and aspiration it has released in the newly regenerated urban quarter.

WHOLE-TOWN VISIONS FOR A DEVELOPMENT PLAN

WICK AND THURSO, SCOTLAND

DATE **FEBRUARY 2012** CLIENT SECTOR **PUBLIC** SITE **URBAN** SCALE **REGION/TOWN**
VISION **PLANNING URBAN DESIGN**

The Highland Council charrettes in Wick and Thurso (sponsored by the Scottish Government) enabled local people to help shape the future growth of their towns. Members of the public and local stakeholders worked in collaboration with council officers and project consultants to develop a vision and masterplan for each town, focused on housing and economic development, including offshore energy. The outcomes from the events were then fed into a new Caithness and Sutherland Local Development Plan process.

'For the council, who wanted to engage a range of people in preparing plans for the area, the charrette events condensed months of work into just a few days. The process led to a step change in the Highland Council's general approach to collaboration and engagement.'

Scott Dalgarno, Manager of the Caithness and Sutherland Local Development Plan

FORESIGHT

Thurso, the most northerly town on the Scottish mainland, overlooks the Pentland Firth and Orkney Islands. Despite having many assets, including a medieval urban core, a world-class surf beach, a railway station and a harbour, Thurso faces a number of economic challenges related in particular to the decommissioning of Dounreay nuclear research establishment, one of the first and once one of the most advanced nuclear research facilities in the world.

Wick is divided by its river, with Wick town centre on the northern bank and Pulteneytown, home of the Old Pulteney whisky distillery, on the southern bank. The town centre contains a significant number

OPPOSITE FIGURE 5.15.1:
Dounreay nuclear research establishment

ABOVE LEFT FIGURE 5.15.2:
Historic image of Wick Harbour

ABOVE RIGHT FIGURE 5.15.3:
Publicity flyer for the Wick charrette

of listed buildings, including the Carnegie Library, laid out on a simple grid around the harbour. At one time Wick Harbour was home to the busiest herring port in Europe. However, with the decline of the old industries Wick also needed to reassess its economic future.

The Scottish Government established the Sustainable Communities Initiative Charrette Mainstreaming Programme in 2011, promoting the use of charrettes to involve local communities in shaping their place. This followed on from the success of three pilot charrettes led by Andrés Duany from Florida-based architects DPZ.

As part of the programme, the Highland Council obtained funding to help in the early stages of preparing the Caithness and Sutherland Local Development Plan. It was an attempt to achieve consensus between as wide a range of partners as possible on the priorities for the future growth in the two main towns in the Caithness and Sutherland plan area, and to create a greater sense of collective ownership and empowerment to deliver the plan and improve communities.

A team was appointed, led by John Thompson & Partners (JTP), with Gillespies, to facilitate the process in Thurso and Wick. The brief was to review key issues facing each town, to explore options and alternatives for delivering development, to propose actions for addressing these issues to deliver growth, and to formulate a land-use strategy. This involved undertaking design-led charrettes in both Thurso (including Scrabster) and Wick, resulting in two whole-town masterplans. The results of the events were to be fed into the first stage of the Caithness and Sutherland Plan, known as the Main Issues Report.

Key stakeholders in Thurso and Wick were invited to launch events, which served to publicise the forthcoming charrettes. Many of those who met with the team agreed to pass on information to colleagues, neighbours and friends. Not everyone, however, was convinced by the use of the terminology 'charrette'. The *John O'Groat Journal* wrote: 'The fact that the events were tagged charrettes was not likely to make them any more appealing to the average Joe. Sounding like a cross between

"charade" and "Tourette's", their esoteric derivation from a practice at a Parisian architecture school was, we thought, hardly going to be a big vote winner.'

Following the launches, and to ensure the widest possible representation from the local community and key stakeholders at the charrettes, a structured programme of engagement (community animation) was undertaken by a team led by community participation expert Dr Geoff Fagan of the CADISPA Trust (Conservation and Development in Sparsely Populated Areas).

VISION
The brief had originally asked for a four-day charrette in each town, but to give the team sufficient time to hold workshops and work on the outputs, it was agreed to blend the charrettes together. This had the benefit of enabling the team to work between the two towns over six days, and learn lessons that could feed into both visions.

The well-attended Thurso workshops were held on 22 and 24 February. Key issues discussed included the future vitality of the heart of the town as a commercial centre, the regeneration and enhancement of the riverside, and the western expansion of the town, including space for employment uses related to the growth of Scrabster Harbour.

Participants also wanted to see new facilities and services to attract further visitors to Thurso, including cultural, heritage and water sports activities.

The Wick workshops on 23 and 24 February were less well attended, and key issues raised included regeneration in the heart of the town on both sides of the river, investment in the harbour, and promoting and investing in Wick as a cultural and heritage visitor destination, as part of a wider Caithness offer.

In both towns, there was an acceptance of the need for new residential and economic development to sustain the community and the economy, and a desire to be seen as part of the Caithness tourism trail.

The charrettes were seen as open and transparent, with high-quality outputs, benefiting from the immediacy of interpreting ideas and concepts into drawings and proposals. However, the relatively low number and range of attendees in Wick led to uncertainty expressed by some over how representative the outputs were.

Following the workshop days, the charrette team analysed and summarised the outcomes, and in consultation with council officers drew up an illustrated vision for each town, and an additional plan for wider Caithness, both of which were reported back to the communities of each town on Day six of each charrette.

HINDSIGHT

The charrette outcomes were welcomed in each town with a great deal of positive energy about development opportunities and the prospect of partnership working to deliver them. In their leader column following the report back presentations, the *John O'Groat Journal* wrote that the projects and initiatives 'were selected and refined by what appeared to be a thoroughly democratic process involving all of the community minded citizens who turned up'. The leader continued: 'We believe this gives the mandate for the project to be taken forward and included within the new development plan for both towns. Anyone who takes issue with the action plans who did not attend can now consider themselves on the back foot as they failed to take up the opportunity to deliver their tuppenceworth.'[19]

Subsequently, the impact of the charrette would have been far greater if the outcome had fed directly into a draft Local Development Plan. The Main Issues Report stage that followed, as dictated by Scottish Government legislation, reopened the debate on sites to be included in the plan, and as a result the outcome of the charrette became more diluted. At the time of writing, the Local Development Plan had reached final examination stage and was being independently assessed by a reporter on behalf of Scottish ministers.

CREATIVE FLOOD PROTECTION INVESTMENT
WHITESANDS, DUMFRIES, SCOTLAND

DATE **SEPTEMBER 2012**   CLIENT SECTOR **PUBLIC**   SITE **URBAN**   SCALE **NEIGHBOURHOOD**
VISION **URBAN DESIGN   GREEN DESIGN**

Creative co-designing of flood protection works to revitalise Whitesands on the banks of the River Nith, the heart of 'The Queen of the South'.

'Working around plans and drawing people's ideas breaks the ice and focuses on the plan – at the end people felt ownership of the ideas.'

Graeme Pert, Gillespies

RIGHT FIGURE 5.16.1:
Whitesands livestock market

BELOW FIGURE 5.16.2:
Whitesands inundated with flood water

FORESIGHT

Dumfries is a historic market town, set in Scotland's Southern Uplands close to the border with England. The fast-flowing River Nith passes through the town on its course to the Solway Firth, and historians trace the earliest settlement at this strategic crossing point back to the Roman era. Through the following centuries Dumfries became a flourishing market town and inland port, and was granted Royal Burgh status by William the Lion in 1186.

In the nineteenth and twentieth centuries various industries established themselves in Dumfries, and the town, which gained the nickname 'The Queen of the South', grew rapidly. Today Dumfries is home to around 40,000 citizens and has established a reputation as one of the best places to live in the UK.

In the twentieth century the closure of the inland port and Whitesands livestock market shifted the town's commercial centre of gravity uphill, away from the river. In addition, the Nith regularly overflowed its banks, causing severe flooding. As a consequence, the blighted Whitesands area came to be characterised by run-down buildings, marginal businesses and empty shops. The uncertainty about the provision of future flood protection was having a negative impact on the regeneration of the area, with knock-on effects on the performance and future planning of the wider town centre.

In August 2012, Dumfries and Galloway Council (DGC) commissioned Gillespies and DG Design to prepare a masterplan for Whitesands. The overarching aims of the study were to address particular flooding issues and increase the vitality of the town centre as a whole.

Whitesands lies within a conservation area and contains a number of listed buildings. The riverside setting, with its historic bridges and streets, is an integral part of the town's heritage. The height and visual impact of any flood barrier within this sensitive environment would therefore need to be carefully planned.

Professor Brian Evans was leader of the project. Having a multidisciplinary team working together over several days is a recognised and effective way of creating integrated solutions to resolve complex problems. As he says: 'It takes leadership to persuade the client to undertake a charrette when, as in Dumfries, the technique had not previously been employed in the area.'

VISION
The team met with the DGC Strategic Projects Group to refine the programme and discuss the anticipated outputs. An introductory workshop was then held with DGC members and town stakeholders to explain the charrette process.

BELOW FIGURE 5.16.3:
Hands-on planning at Whitesands charrette

'The Future of the Whitesands' charrette took place between 12 and 19 September 2012 at a town centre hotel, and involved a series of interactive presentations, dialogue workshops, walkabouts and design workshops, as well as meetings with all stakeholders to discuss the key policies and issues relating to the site.

The collaborative process enabled members of the public, local design professionals and project consultants to work together to develop a detailed vision for the site. Particular effort was made to talk with business owners at Whitesands, and on the Saturday a market stall was set up to seek the views of town centre users.

Throughout the charrette participants were able to walk around the area in groups, looking at key views and the various conditions along the banks of the river. This opportunity for observation, along with discussion of issues and opportunities, was fundamental to the success of the process.

It soon became evident that the technical vocabulary and complexity of flood risk issues was difficult but vital for local decision-makers and members of the community to grasp. Many hours were spent explaining and discussing concepts such as 1-in-25- and 1-in-100-year flood risks. The charrette process allowed time for this kind of detailed discussion, which was critical in order to reach understanding and agreement on the most appropriate risk level to plan for.

The site area incorporated the existing riverside car parks and bus terminus, and the vision showed these transformed into a new multiuse, high-amenity landscape. As one participant commented, 'Why should the cars have the best view?' Whitesands would provide a place of arrival for visitors by bus, cycle and car, and the green landscape and 'cafe society' quality of the new Whitesands riverfront would complement the commercial and civic role of the High Street. The secondary streets between the two parallel

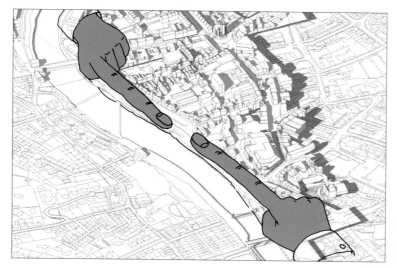

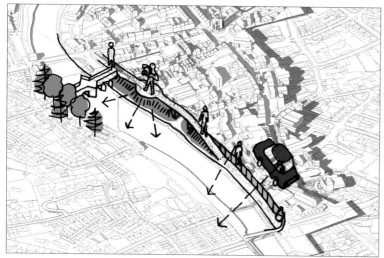

ABOVE FIGURES 5.16.4 & 5.16.4A:
**Cartoon drawings
explaining concepts for
the Whitesands vision**

thoroughfares would be revitalised by the heritage-led regeneration of the surviving building fabric and remaining medieval patterns of plot shapes, wynds and closes.

The leafy, countrified riverbanks immediately upstream and downstream from Whitesands were extended into the town centre, with both banks becoming a tree-lined setting for the River Nith.

Key to everything, it was agreed that the level of protection adopted for Whitesands should be at least for a 1-in-25-year flood event. This would allow a significant degree of confidence to return to this part of the town centre while avoiding the considerable nuisance of regular flooding and allowing insurance cover to be explored.

Where width allowed, the method of flood protection was to be a landscape bund behind the existing riverbank wall and riverside walkway. At the top of the bund an elevated walkway would give enhanced views of the river.

HINDSIGHT
Following the charrette, further design development that offered greater than the 1-in-25-year protection was explored, to seek better protection without significantly compromising views and to reflect Scottish Environmental Protection Agency guidance. Regular meetings were held with key stakeholders, and a series of community events were arranged to share the emerging proposals. These well-publicised and well-attended events revealed a high level of satisfaction with the clarity and relevance of display materials and the process in general, a good understanding of the issues, and a high level of general support for the proposals.

At the second exhibition many people commented that the proposed new flood protection embankment was now too high in places. This concern led to a redesign of the scheme and a resultant reduction of the overall height of the embankment to a

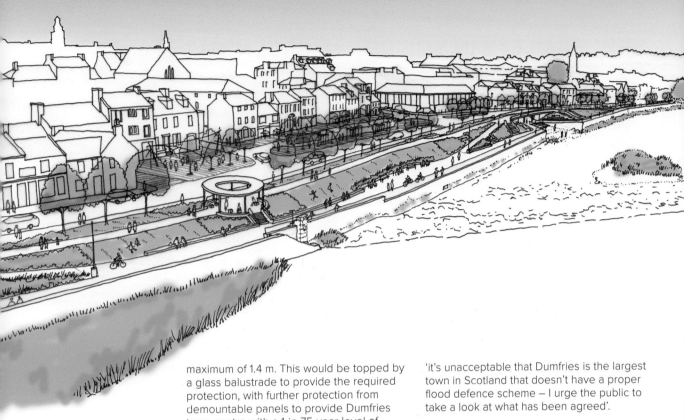

maximum of 1.4 m. This would be topped by a glass balustrade to provide the required protection, with further protection from demountable panels to provide Dumfries town centre with a 1-in-75-year level of protection.

However, support has not been universal, and concern among some businesses in the Whitesands area about the disruption during construction and the loss of parking in the immediate area has led to a campaign against the proposals. While these concerns were heard through the charrette and measures were taken to mitigate the impacts, the campaign demonstrates that sometimes not everyone will be satisfied with the outcomes despite the consensus-building process. Not everyone takes the opportunity to get involved at an early stage, for whatever reason, and so may not go through the process of dialogue and confronting difficult choices. The response from Colin Smyth, Chairman of the Environment, Economy and Infrastructure Committee at DGC was that

'it's unacceptable that Dumfries is the largest town in Scotland that doesn't have a proper flood defence scheme – I urge the public to take a look at what has been agreed'.

In 2015, three years after the charrette, the scheme to provide flood protection and regeneration for the Whitesands area was unanimously approved by the council. At the time of writing, the £25m scheme, based on a raised walkway concept with a combination of walls, glass balustrades, demountable panels and floodgates, will be submitted formally to the Scottish Government, advising them of the preliminary decision to confirm the scheme without modifications.

NEW HAMLETS IN THE RURAL GREENBELT
CADDINGTON, BEDFORDSHIRE, ENGLAND

DATE **APRIL 2013** CLIENT SECTOR **PRIVATE** SITE **RURAL** SCALE **NEIGHBOURHOOD**
VISION **URBAN DESIGN GREEN DESIGN GOVERNANCE**

A partnership approach between private, public and community sectors resulted in innovative and sensitive proposals for mixed-tenure housing in the rural greenbelt, with community facilities, green infrastructure and a new bus service all managed by a Community Trust.

'There was enormous benefit in the hot-housing of ideas over five days with a range of stakeholders, which ultimately garnered support. GM Vauxhall selected the right set of skills in terms of their advisors — they put investment into understanding the issues first, rather than just hammering in a planning application. Big developments can be carried through with local support.'

Councillor Richard Stay, former Deputy Leader of Central Bedfordshire Council and local ward member

FORESIGHT

Caddington Woods (formerly known by the working title 'Chaulington') is a 27-hectare (67-acre) site in rural Bedfordshire, originally constructed by General Motors Vauxhall as a vehicle testing track. It was then used as a place to store vehicles assembled at the Luton factory. By 2013, as manufacturing processes evolved, such a large storage site was no longer needed.

The site was considered potentially suitable for residential development, which would help Central Bedfordshire Council meet its housing need. However, given the site's greenbelt setting, any such planning application would have to successfully demonstrate 'very special circumstances'.

For GM Vauxhall, which had been part of the local scene for over 100 years, redevelopment of the site was a reputational issue. The firm was keen to deliver something of high quality as a legacy to the area. With this in mind, Julian Lyon, GM Vauxhall's European Real Estate Manager, approached Central Bedfordshire Council to discuss the site's future.

Councillor Richard Stay, former Deputy Leader of Central Bedfordshire Council and local ward member, remembers the occasion: 'Julian contacted me and said he would like to have a conversation. We went down for a meeting and started a very successful partnership — over many months we arrived at something quite unique.' Kevin Collins, Chair of the Slip End and Caddington Neighbourhood Plan Forum, was at the same meeting: 'The assumption was that it would be housing, and we said

we didn't want lots of high-density housing — we wanted something that would fit with the rural community.'

GM appointed a team, led by CBRE, with a view to using a community planning process, facilitated by John Thompson & Partners (JTP), to develop a vision for the site.

VISION
After an initial meeting with community representatives at the Chaul End golf club, a sequence of steering group meetings was held to involve the community in the organisation of the 'New Vision for Chaulington Community Planning Weekend'. Kevin Collins recalls how helpful it was for the Neighbourhood Plan Forum to be actively involved. With its links to the community, it meant that more people were encouraged to come along and participate.

In the run-up to the charrette, Debbie Radcliffe, one of the team members, spent time cycling around the area, researching its history and meeting with members of the community in organised and ad hoc ways.

The charrette was held in April 2013. It began with public workshops, held over two days, which gave participants the opportunity to share local knowledge and contribute to planning the future of the site. Alison Tero from CBRE recalls the welcoming atmosphere: 'Everybody, of whatever age or role, was able to express their views and ideas — the facilitators set the tone.'

A key element of the event was the opportunity to visit the site in a minibus. This enabled people to see first-hand its special characteristics before they participated in co-design hands-on planning workshops. In most cases it changed people's perception from 'this is greenbelt' to 'this is a concrete car park', and — more importantly — that 'this is a screened site'.

TOP RIGHT FIGURE 5.17.2:
String of villages and hamlets along a ridge

BELOW LEFT FIGURE 5.17.3:
Hands-on planning group report back on emerging concepts

BELOW RIGHT FIGURE 5.17.4:
Vignette of the village green with duck pond

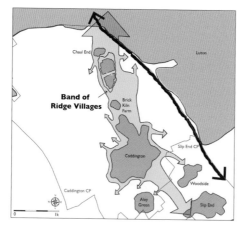

The charrette team worked in a nearby hotel over the next three days to draw up the vision for the site. The illustrated masterplan showed a new development of around 325 homes divided into two hamlets, to maintain the integrity of the 'string of villages', with a range of house types reflecting local architectural styles and layouts, all set in a high-quality managed landscape. A village green with duck pond and a multiuse community building were located between the two hamlets. This provided a focus for the new communities, which were all connected to the bridleway and footpath network of the surrounding area.

The hands-on planning sessions created clear concepts for the site. It was to be a distinct new settlement, part of the string of villages and hamlets located along a ridge, well connected to Caddington village to the south, with complementary, not competing, community facilities. Transport was also a key issue, and a proposal to provide a new subsidised bus service emerged during the charrette.

HINDSIGHT

In the months following the charrette, the team drew up an outline planning application for the site, including a design code and demonstrating 'very special circumstances'. Through this stage the residential team from CBRE market-tested the proposals with a range of developers so that when the application was submitted the team were confident it was fit for purpose.

EXISTING WATER BODY RECONFIGURED TO CREATE POND AS FOCAL POINT TO VILLAGE GREEN OVERLOOKED BY NEW HOUSING

CHADLINGTON
APRIL 2013

The charrette process had shown how the development could meet community needs and aspirations, while minimising impact on the greenbelt. Councillor Stay explains: 'All the debate and dialogue enabled us to engage with our own planners, and the overall scheme went through planning with the support of the council.'

Once planning had been granted, the site was bought by housebuilder Redrow. At the time of writing the first phase of the new 'Caddington Woods' has been built and occupied, and a Community Trust is being established which will own forty-four homes in perpetuity, generating an annual rental income of over £300,000 to fund operations. These include running a new bus service, managing the multifunctional community building, and looking after the shared open space and woodland around the development.

As initiator of the process, Julian Lyon reflects that 'the charrette brought together many local people with different ages and backgrounds who found a real sense of what was possible. The principles developed at the workshops remained throughout our planning and sale process as the fundamental values and parameters for the development'.

THE BIG BARNES PONDER
BARNES, LONDON, ENGLAND

DATE **OCTOBER 2013**   CLIENT SECTOR **COMMUNITY**   SITE **URBAN**
SCALE **NEIGHBOURHOOD**   VISION **URBAN DESIGN GOVERNANCE**

An affluent suburban village community worked with
professionals to address the decline of their High Street and
create a holistic vision for the area's future, and action teams to
deliver it.

'We had to learn from the professionals and the placemaking agenda
has helped us crystallise our thinking about the way we look at the
village: the shops, the traffic and the footfall. Traders are more aware
now of what they need to do to run a successful business. And the
community at large is now more aware of the usefulness of the High
Street – if they don't use it, they'll lose it.'

Steven Mindel, Chair, Barnes Community Association

FORESIGHT

Barnes is a leafy and prosperous suburban
village surrounded to the north by a loop
of the River Thames and to the south by
Barnes Common. St Mary's parish church
dates back approximately 900 years to
Norman times, and the village has evolved
over the centuries from being truly rural to
now forming the neighbourhood heart for
around 8,000 homes.

In 2010 to 2011 the High Street was in
trouble, with empty retail units and low
footfall threatening the survival of well-

RIGHT FIGURE 5.18.1:
**Barnes Pond – the
focal point of the
community**

TOP LEFT FIGURE 5.18.2:
Nick Taylor from Scarborough, Barnes Town Centre Manager Emma Robinson and local MP Zac Goldsmith at the Barnes Ponder charrette

TOP RIGHT FIGURE 5.18.3:
Workshop wall at the end of the session

established independent shops. The situation was blamed on a combination of factors, including changes in shopping patterns, high rents and business rates, lack of ready cash following the credit crunch, and the dominance of traffic in the High Street, which created an uncomfortable environment.

Inspired by two community-based initiatives, Incredible Edible in Todmorden, Yorkshire and The People's Supermarket in Camden, London, a group of Barnes residents came together to see what could be done, and eventually established a group called 'Everyday Barnes'.

Around this time, the UK's coalition government commissioned retail expert Mary Portas to undertake a review of high streets in England. One of the recommendations was that communities should establish Town Teams to drive innovation and improvements in their high streets.

A new Town Team was formed, and it was decided that the first step was to consult with the local community to create a vision for Barnes as a brief for future initiatives. It was agreed that a one-day charrette should be held called 'The Big Barnes Ponder', a pun on the local landmark of Barnes Pond.

To enable the creation of a holistic vision, the project was to be given a broad social and environmental remit, and not just cover retail and high street issues.

VISION

Members of the Town Team agreed to take on tasks to organise and publicise the Ponder, which was launched two weeks before the charrette took place, by attracting young families with free face-painting for children and with huge pink bows tied to trees on Barnes Green. The Ponder was also widely publicised through local media including Barnes Community Association (BCA) *Prospect* magazine and the *Barnes Bugle*. This all created a great deal of interest and started people talking about the future of the village neighbourhood.

The Big Barnes Ponder was held on Saturday 19 October 2013. It was facilitated by a team of professionals, working on an expenses-only basis.

The charrette started early in the morning with a team tour of Barnes, organised by local resident and professional guide Sue Boyd. While this was happening, Ponder volunteers set up the venue with a background exhibition, workshop seating and refreshments donated by local businesses.

Around eleven o'clock the Barnes community, including local Member of Parliament Zac Goldsmith, began to arrive to sign in, view the exhibition and take their seats for the workshop. After a brief introduction, the first sticky-note workshop commenced, with participants asked to consider and write down their issues, dreams and solutions for Barnes. This stimulated ninety minutes of active and progressive debate among the community.

The resulting themes influenced the topics for the afternoon hands-on planning session. Six table groups focused on issues such as Getting About Barnes, Barnes Green to the River, Community Facilities and The High Street. Good-natured conversation and peals of laughter filled the room as people debated and sketched their ideas on to plans.

Zac Goldsmith recalls: 'I very much enjoyed the Ponder – the approach was getting people actively involved – bottom up has always been the best approach.'

By splitting into different work groups individuals could choose which ideas they had a passion for, look into these in more

depth, and then report back findings to everyone attending the session.

People started to see a huge desire emerging to improve the village, draw the community closer together and create a more vibrant commercial environment. The public sessions finished with a way forward workshop discussion on how to move projects along and draw in more participation.

At the end of the day the facilitation team held a debriefing meeting, fuelled by pizzas donated by a local restaurant. The team worked over the following days to distil the community vision, which was drawn up and reported back to the community ten days later to a packed hall.

HINDSIGHT

Three years on, Steven Mindel, who was active in the organisation of the charrette, had become BCA Chair. He reflects on the process: 'You cannot downplay the importance of the Ponder – people like to talk to people. I loved the workshops and all the Post-it notes. Even with today's sophisticated communication technology, until you speak to someone face to face and get the measure of the person you can't do business with them.'

A key outcome from the Ponder was the setting up of six Ponder Action Teams to develop identified projects, which included a 20's Plenty campaign to reduce speed limits, a new branding and marketing exercise for the village, and environmental improvements for Suffolk Road Recreation Ground, the High Street and along the river.

Perhaps most crucially, Steven believes that the Ponder short-circuited the idea of a Neighbourhood Plan. It was undertaken with the input of experts working with the community but with nowhere near as much effort and without the cost. He says: 'A Neighbourhood Plan can cost £60,000 to £100,000 – the Ponder was put on for just £3,000 and a lot of goodwill.'

BELOW FIGURE 5.18.4:
Vision for closing Barnes High Street to traffic on festival and market days

ABOVE FIGURE 5.18.5:
New Barnes marketing logo – 'Barnes: a welcome escape'

BELOW FIGURE 5.18.6:
Vision for the new Barnes Garden Bridge

In response to the creation of the Ponder Vision, Richmond Council brought forward the creation of a Village Plan for Barnes, which now acts as Supplementary Planning Guidance.

A visit to Barnes High Street today reveals a very different place. There is a healthy mix of national chains and independent shops, cafes and pubs, which creates a vibrant retail and community hub. An increased awareness of the High Street has encouraged people to support local shops and businesses and take part in a wide range of community and cultural activities. The new Olympic cinema, refurbished by a local couple, has created a magnet at one end of the High Street, and the recently opened M&S Foodhall is a draw at the opposite end. The result is a significant leap in footfall.

The Ponder projects are starting to bear fruit. The council has invested £20,000 in a placemaking study of the High Street/Church Road corridor. There is also a focus on Suffolk Road Recreation Ground, and funds have been set aside and a friends' group established to drive through improvements.

Ambitious long-term plans are focusing on creating a new garden bridge on a disused part of Barnes Bridge, boardwalks along the river, and opening up new spaces for people to enjoy.

In 2016, three years after the participatory Ponder, Barnes was rated 'the hippest village in West London' by a local property magazine, demonstrating that when a community comes together with a unity of purpose, much can be achieved from within the community and by attracting outside investment.

The charrette enabled local people to create a community-led vision for the future of their village, and Emma Robinson, Barnes Town Centre Manager, agrees: 'The approach to the event encouraged residents to think creatively about their dreams.' At the time of writing, Ponder teams are still energised and working to deliver key projects with broad community support. Those at the centre of delivering the vision trace the origins of the village renaissance back to the open, participatory Big Barnes Ponder, a process run with very limited financial resources, but which released huge amounts of community goodwill and social capital.

DESIGNING COMMUNITY GOVERNANCE FOR A NEW TOWN

LIANGZHU CULTURAL VILLAGE, HANGZHOU, CHINA

DATE **JUNE 2015**   CLIENT SECTOR **PRIVATE**   SITE **URBAN**   SCALE **TOWN**   VISION **GOVERNANCE**

A new vision was created to enable the community of a new garden town named Liangzhu Cultural Village, on a site from the 5,000-year-old Liangzhu jade culture, one of the world's great civilisations, to develop a new structure for self-governance and a charter for the future – 5000+1.

'We want to solve problems rather than cause conflict between the developer and us. Instead of depending on the developer to solve problems for us, we should consider solving the problems by ourselves ... We need a Village Dream – a dream with shared values.'

Local resident

FORESIGHT

The Liangzhu culture was one of the world's great ancient civilisations, known for its city building, advanced agricultural practices and intricately worked jade and other artefacts. The culture inhabited the wetland plain of the Yangtze River Delta between Daxiong Mountain and the Dazhe Mountains. The Liangzhu Ancient City is said to have been the largest city during this time, with an internal area of 290 hectares (more than 700 acres), and surrounded by clay walls, with six city gates.

Archaeological finds date the culture to around 5,000 years ago, but the lack of finds more recent than 4,500 years old has led researchers to believe that the culture's demise was brought about by extreme environmental changes, possibly caused by a meteor impact, which led to the flooding of the plain on which it is situated.

In November 2007 the Zhejiang provincial government announced the discovery of relics related to the city wall, which located the site at the centre of the Liangzhu culture. Architect David Chipperfield was commissioned to design the new Liangzhu Culture Museum, which was completed and opened in 2008.

Liangzhu Cultural Village is a new garden town located in Hangzhou's Yuhang District, about 20 kilometres (12 miles) away from Hangzhou city centre. Vanke, China's largest developer, started construction in 2000 and, in stark contrast to the myriad high-rise towers of Hangzhou, Liangzhu Cultural Village is a mix of apartment blocks and houses set in a stunning landscape. As

OPPOSITE FIGURE 5.19.1:
**Exhibit at the Liangzhu
Culture Museum**

RIGHT FIGURE 5.19.2:
**Liangzhu Cultural
Village central street**

well as the museum, the village boasts a variety of attractions, including shops and restaurants, a church, a cultural centre and a children's park. By 2015 the population had reached over 10,000, with an additional 40,000 new citizens planned by 2022. In a conscious attempt to create a strong civil society the planners drew up a 'village treaty', a document signed by Liangzhu's 3,000 households. The town has been recognised as an exemplar town in China.

During the early life of the new town, Vanke had acted as the town council, running and maintaining the physical and social infrastructure of the town. But, as part of its exit strategy from the town, Vanke wanted to assess the achievements of the town so far and discuss with the residents the key issues of its future development, including the town's long-term management and governance.

VISION
Commissioned by the Vanke Group, JTP held a Community Planning Weekend at Hangzhou Liangzhu Cultural Village in June 2015. The event lasted five days, and included participatory workshops for invited residents.

Following a team briefing day on the Friday, more than seventy villagers joined the weekend workshops. These began on the Saturday afternoon with an introduction to the international experience of the facilitation team and the aim of the event. Residents then participated in a discussion workshop facilitated by the local Chinese-speaking team to talk about issues, dreams and solutions for the town. The UK-based team members had headsets that conveyed simultaneous translation into English.

During the workshops one of the participants, Mr Shen, a resident and manager of the project, gave a presentation to stimulate debate. The presentation included the need for a town vision to create a beautiful, social and welcoming town, models for town governance and options for funding a new town council.

Initially, residents were invited to talk about their 'problems', and this drew out, as intended, some negative issues from participants, including some directed towards Vanke. But then one of the residents suggested that rather than being

BELOW LEFT FIGURE 5.19.3:
**Hands-on planning
group working**

BELOW RIGHT FIGURE 5.19.4:
**Hands-on planning
report back**

negative the participants should be working together to solve problems. From this point, the atmosphere became more harmonious and constructive.

On the Sunday morning, residents participated in three hands-on planning groups around plans of the new town. The themes were 'Transportation, landscape and ecology', 'Community self-management organisation' and 'Community facilities – education, culture, art, hospital, etc.'. Participants chose which table to join, and drew out their ideas with the help of the JTP facilitation team. At the end of the session, each table selected a representative to present their group's ideas, which revealed the wide depth and breadth of their thinking.

After the Sunday workshop, the JTP team, client and representatives of the residents met again to agree the consensus from the event. This included drawing up a programme of action for one week, three months and six months in order to solve the key issues that residents had brought up. During this session the concept of '5000+1' was developed to describe the new future for Liangzhu Cutural Village, which built on the Liangzhu culture's 5,000-year history.

The JTP team worked for the next three days to bring together recommendations for the future of the Cultural Village, which was reported back on Day five of the Community Planning Weekend.

As a first step, it was explained that local residents wanted a platform for better communication to work towards a better, more beautiful Liangzhu. They also wanted to plan more community amenities and services, better integration of visitors and residents, and a new town charter and governance structure for the longer term.

HINDSIGHT
By initiating a collaborative planning process, Vanke as the developer enabled and created an environment of genuine engagement and interaction in which, through honest and open dialogue, consensus could be developed. At the time of writing, two years on from the Community Planning Weekend, a range of new initiatives are in place or being developed. Most importantly for the long-term future of the town, a Community Trust has been established, which will deliver a sustainable governance structure for the community.

'Quick wins' have included the promotion of

THANK YOU!　谢谢！

ABOVE FIGURE 5.19.5:
Participants at the charrette

the town's identity through the production of an artist-designed 'villager fan', 'villager T-shirt' and other items. There are also more than forty active interest groups, such as a new mum's group and a foodie group. The elderly people's quarter is thriving, with a range of activities focusing on elderly people and their families.

The Liangzhu Centre of Arts, designed by Japanese architect Tadao Ando, is now open as a place for Liangzhu villagers to gather together for talks, events and sharing sessions. Mr Shen advises that most community events are still organised by Vanke. It may be some time before the community runs the centre, but there is a positive belief that this time will come.

At the end of the Community Planning Weekend the community was highly motivated and expressed a desire to take more responsibility for managing the town together with the developer and the government. The process injected great confidence and spirit into the community, enabling it to move forward.

AN ALTERNATIVE VISION FOR PADDINGTON PLACE
PADDINGTON, LONDON, ENGLAND

DATE **MAY 2016**   CLIENT SECTOR **THIRD**   SITE **URBAN**   SCALE **NEIGHBOURHOOD** VISION **URBAN DESIGN**

A charrette process was used as a quick and effective way to create an alternative community-backed vision for a masterplan-based approach to a controversial development proposal.

'It's a refreshing change to have the people who know the area really well – how it works, how it could work so much better – being able to share their knowledge and passion with the placemaking professionals who can bring it all together in a far more friendly and practical scheme, where people will not only want to be, but will also want to come to. It's great how much of what we said has been captured in the vision.'

Sue Nichols, South East Bayswater Residents' Association

FORESIGHT

In January 2016, following a public outcry, the proposal for a seventy-two-storey tower designed by Renzo Piano, nicknamed the 'Paddington Pole', was withdrawn. The Great Western Developments Ltd scheme had sought to create a new 'gateway' for Paddington station and neighbouring St Mary's Hospital, deliver improvements to the Network Rail and tube stations, and provide housing and commercial uses as well as new public realm.

MAIN FIGURE 5.20.1:
View from Paddington station to the former Royal Mail sorting office

RIGHT FIGURE 5.20.2:
Consensus masterplan

BELOW RIGHT FIGURE 5.20.3:
Design workshop

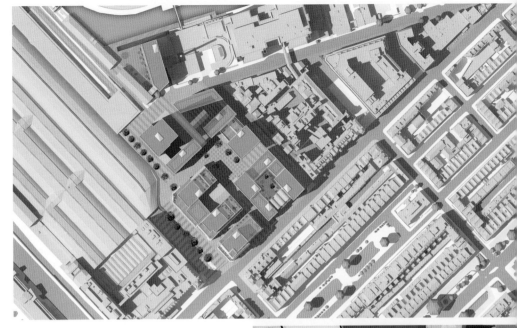

Create Streets, a thinktank focusing on towns and cities, launched an open ideas competition to find a new high-quality alternative scheme for Paddington to encourage public debate and influence future proposals. The competition site area was bigger than that of the Paddington Pole proposal to encourage a more integrated and strategic masterplanning approach.

The site lies next to one of the city's most important train stations – Paddington, with its Grade I listed train shed. It is also close to conservation areas, historic buildings and Royal Parks.

Architects JTP teamed up with Civic Voice, the national charity for the civic movement in England, to hold a Community Planning Weekend to demonstrate how the participatory charrette process, involving the community working with professionals, could create viable alternative proposals for a complex inner-city site over a few days. Civic Voice has a network of over 75,000 individual members and its mission is the development of a society where everyone can say 'I care about where I live'.

People movement experts Movement Strategies and crowd movement analysts Disperse also joined the team.

VISION

Over the course of the May Day bank holiday, local people and others with an interest in the future of Paddington were invited to participate in two days of workshops and walkabouts to create a new vision for the site and its relationship with the surrounding area. They shared their ideas to the design team through walkabouts, workshops and hands-on planning groups.

The community were supportive of the comprehensive, mixed-use regeneration of this important area – but they wanted to see the site planned in a historically sensitive manner and at an appropriate scale to create an attractive, vibrant new heart for Paddington.

Other themes to emerge from the process were that:

- **The Praed Street station entrance could become a high-quality public space**

- **Improved routes and public spaces could contribute to regeneration**

- **Housing for people of all income levels should have a place**

- **Value should be attached to existing local residential and business communities**

- **Redevelopment of the site needed to relate to St Mary's Hospital**

- **There was an opportunity to redistribute pedestrian and traffic flows**

- **The regeneration of Praed Street could be helped by this site.**

These themes were central to the design produced by the JTP team following the Community Planning Weekend. After a few days of intensive team working, the consensus vision was reported back to the community on 3 May 2016.

The design proposals reflected the desire for an integrated and animated network of streets and spaces for Paddington Place. In this respect the local community's wishes corresponded to the timeless principles of walkable urbanism and sustainable placemaking.

Following the presentation, the vision was submitted as the entry to the Create Streets design competition.

HINDSIGHT

JTP and Civic Voice were awarded joint first prize for their competition entry. Sophie Massey Cook, one of the judges, said: 'We were impressed by the level of community participation undertaken in such a short timeframe. We were also impressed by the urban fabric, and the quality of the public spaces and blocks.'

The prizes were awarded by journalist Sir Simon Jenkins at a ceremony in July 2016.

Nicholas Boys Smith, of the thinktank, concluded: 'Civic Voice and JTP's submission shows that you can work rapidly and productively with a local community to achieve intense and potentially beautiful urban development proposals. With widespread coverage in the London media the Paddington Pole competition helped move the debate on from simple opposition to oversized development to pragmatic support for a street-based alternative.'

In the months following the competition a new proposal designed by Renzo Piano was unveiled by the developers for a nineteen-storey office building, which was given the nickname the Paddington Cube. Although the scheme evoked further criticism, including for its design and the lack of housing, many people felt that some elements, particularly in relation to the public realm and pedestrian movement, had been improved. Despite a further campaign against the new scheme and many objections, planning approval was granted by Westminster City Council in early 2017.

CHAPTER | 6
LESSONS FROM THE CASE STUDIES

'It is time to change the way things are done and to bring communities genuinely to the heart of planning and placemaking. "Participation not Consultation" is about bringing people in at an early stage to develop the proposals through collaborative planning processes, also known as charrettes.'

GRIFF RHYS JONES, PRESIDENT, CIVIC VOICE

1

GLOBAL RELEVANCE

Charrettes can work in any community around the world. The case studies demonstrate that successful charrette processes have been run in cultures and places as diverse as Australia and Iceland, China and the Middle East, Canada and Germany, and they prove that culture and context is no barrier to a successful process.

Nevertheless, there are several practical aspects that should be considered. Charrettes should always be run in the local language to ensure local participation is not impeded by the use of a second language. International teams can still lead charrettes when simultaneous translation is provided. The use of sketching and visualisation also overcomes barriers of language and literacy.

For practitioners working in culturally unfamiliar contexts it is essential to undertake social and historical research. Getting to know community leaders first will help this understanding, build trust and give access to the wider community. The potential for preliminary 'community animation' work and the number and choice of workshop participants during the charrette may be limited by local political considerations.

2

SCALE AND TYPES OF PROJECT

Charrettes can be tailored to any scale and type of built environment project, from town or regional planning to neighbourhood revitalisation and the design of buildings.

Charrettes are known for attracting wide public involvement and are programmed to include public and team-working sessions. In some cases, the technical complexity of the project may result in a more specifically structured programme, with communities and professionals coming together at different stages of the process. In Liverpool at Alder Hey, for example, this took the form of distinct workshops for technical experts and the general public, but everything was handled as part of the same overall process, which ensured the integration and the respect of inputs from members of the community.

Where there is no community in and around the site area, or the charrette is organised as a particular method of technical team working, the benefits of cross-discipline, multiday team working on site can still apply.

3

NON-CONFRONTATIONAL EXPLORATION OF IDEAS WITH INDEPENDENT FACILITATION

Charrettes create a non-confrontational forum for ideas to be introduced and discussed. The structure of a charrette's process encourages the rigour of debate within an informal environment through independent facilitation. Workshops never take the form of lectures with facts to be absorbed in silence; rather they are places for suggestions and disagreements, evolving attitudes and changes of mind.

A charrette is a people-focused process, and people can and do differ in outlook and experience. The independence of the facilitators helps the management of the event and allows a process where arguments can arise and be resolved, where difficult development scenarios can be examined. It is a process through which people recognise that a good idea is a good idea and it matters not whether it came from an individual or emerged from group working.

Although the original motivation for a collaborative planning exercise could be a new neighbourhood development proposal such as Gardebær, Iceland or the exploration of a new public realm strategy such as Lübeck, in each instance the freedom of expression allows best practice ideas to be aired and developed. These can take projects into territory that may be unfamiliar to members of the community but result in innovative and leading-edge outcomes, and ultimately more integrated, sustainable solutions.

4
SPECIFIC-ISSUE CHARRETTES CAN CATALYSE WIDER PLACEMAKING VISIONS

By taking a holistic, placemaking approach to the site concerned, the initial stimulus for the charrette becomes a catalyst for the wider revitalisation of an area and be supported by all. This in turn generates new initiatives and a sense of momentum. In Dunedin, for example, earthquake-strengthening legislation provided the momentum for wider regeneration. New community champions can emerge, and the baton from a single-issue-inspired event is passed on to a much wider audience.

The case studies include charrettes that were held for specific purposes, such as post-tornado recovery (East Nashville), addressing economic decline (Scarborough), agreeing flood protection works (Dumfries) and the introduction of earthquake-strengthening legislation (Dunedin).

5
COMMISSIONING BODY – PRIVATE, PUBLIC, COMMUNITY

Charrettes are appropriate for private, public and community sector-led projects, and the case studies give examples of charrettes commissioned by all three sectors, such as River District, Vancouver (private), Midland, Perth (public) and Paddington Place, London (community).

Early involvement of the community in projects that will affect their place is important in bringing local knowledge into the process and building support, regardless of who has commissioned the project. It is the focus on 'Place' and the people who use it that is key to changing perceptions and creating consensus.

Which body commissions the charrette is likely to have an impact on the budget available, but the case studies demonstrate that charrettes can work effectively when properly organised and resourced, across a full range of budgets.

There are certain directives that should always be followed, such as drafting and publicising a clear mission statement for the charrette, independent facilitation, and an open and transparent process.

6
POLITICIANS AND STAKEHOLDERS

Planning processes are more than likely at some stage to require the involvement of politicians and statutory organisations. While charrettes are apolitical planning processes, political decision-makers and stakeholders should be communicated with in the early stages of organising a charrette process, so that they are fully briefed about its timing and objectives. This can be done effectively through early meetings or inviting stakeholders to an event to launch the process. It would undermine the process should they hear about it second-hand, perhaps from a constituent or colleague.

Case studies at Caddington and Wick and Thurso show how early working with local politicians and stakeholders helped set the trajectory of the process. In Caddington early political and stakeholder engagement helped ensure effective event organisation and community participation. At Wick and Thurso inviting politicians and stakeholders to the launch event gave the local authority-backed process proactive and widespread media coverage.

The presence and involvement of politicians is usually expected and welcomed by the local community at charrettes, as long as politicians respect the collaborative, consensus-led nature of the process, and do not grandstand or try to score political points.

7

COMMUNITY INVOLVEMENT IN ORGANISATION

Many of the case studies benefited from the close involvement of members of the community to organise the event itself. The participation of local people at the start ensures the event is appropriately organised, programmed and publicised. Although facilitation by multiskilled professionals is key, the collaborative nature of a charrette allows for the community to be positively engaged and stimulated by the inherent potential of the participatory process.

The best publicity is word of mouth, and excitement can be contagious. At Lübeck, Germany the *Unterstützerkreis* (steering group) had input into key decisions about the organisation of the process and helped ensure wide publicity throughout the city. The participation of over 400 people in the process led to innovative and well-supported outcomes.

8

CREATIVE BUSINESS COMMUNITIES

It is important to include the local business community and creative sector in the charrette process. This can be difficult – traders and businesspeople often work long hours, and may consider that planning is not relevant to their endeavours. From a practical point of view, it may be necessary to tailor the timing of workshops to suit the working hours of such groups.

However, entrepreneurship and culture is the lifeblood of a healthy community and, as the Scarborough and Dunedin processes demonstrate, active participation by these sectors can create momentum in the process and unexpected investment opportunities. Exploiting specific local artistic talent can enliven a charrette process and emphasise its local distinctiveness, such as in the Blaenau Ffestiniog regeneration.

It may be possible to involve the creative business community in delivering 'quick wins', activities or events to generate interest and maintain momentum in a regeneration process, which can take many years to deliver physical results.

There are positive gains to be made by actively involving the creative community in the delivery of short-term projects. These generate excitement and show that change can be positive – and fun. Engagement with local businesses can inspire people to become ambassadors for change. Small steps and low-key initiatives can lead to the creation of thriving and vibrant places.

9

COMMUNITY ANIMATION

Charrettes are most effective, and valuable, when the resulting consensus vision has involved the widest possible cross-section of the community.

A well-resourced charrette preparation period, such as in Scarborough, helps to animate all sections of the community and lead to wide-ranging participation. Meeting local individuals and groups ahead of the charrette using established networks uncovers local issues, cuts through any scepticism about the process and encourages involvement, ensuring a balanced perspective. Information-gathering is also part of the pre-charrette process, and pre-event gleanings add to the input of local knowledge.

In several case studies, including Santa Fe and Kew Bridge, members of the team spent time getting to know the community and their concerns through both organised and ad hoc meetings. Effort is needed to encourage participation across a wide spectrum of the population, and working with hard-to-reach groups, especially the younger generation, can produce stimulating and unexpected results.

10
LEARNING AND CAPACITY BUILDING

Charrettes increase knowledge, confidence and capacity building within a community. The workshops can help moderate behaviour, change perceptions and awaken aspirations. Charrettes create a valuable win-win situation, as the outside professionals gain insight from the locals, and locals acquire new knowledge and experience.

Local people know their place well, from a personal perspective, but may have little knowledge of the principles of urban design and how to express often complex ideas. One of the major benefits of holding a charrette is the knowledge exchange that occurs during the public event. The role played by outside facilitators is crucial. They need to pass on technical knowledge and be willing to learn from the community as local experts. This can include formal presentations before and during the charrette including principles of good urbanism, understanding viability, an assessment of the local context, and so on. As a result, local people of all ages and from all walks of life can begin to understand or appreciate the assets of their community in a different way.

11
DIALOGUE AND FEEDBACK LOOPS

Dialogue and feedback loops are key elements of charrette processes. They enable complex issues to be communicated and debated in order to make decisions and develop effective and supportive solutions, together with a growing awareness that some compromises are necessary. Talking and sketching together helps to ensure that written and drawn solutions reflect the issues and ideas discussed.

At Alder Hey the community allowed building in their park by collaboratively designing a land swap which allowed for a new, reoriented and better-equipped park in the future.

Charrettes help people to prioritise community needs and desires and work out how to achieve them. For example, value-generating uses, such as residential housing, may create funds needed to subsidise community benefits, such as creative workspace or bus services. Cross-funding initiatives can therefore incorporate community aspirations into the vision, but there must be a willingness, on all sides, to have honest and transparent dialogue about the issues and solutions.

The Caterham Barracks charrette is an example of how the community accepted that the facilities they wanted could only be possible if there was an increase in housing, and that this must be well designed and well laid out.

12
RESPECT AND TRUST

Most charrette attendees volunteer their time, and the client and facilitation team must accept the essential right of the community to be involved. Local people are experts of the place in which they live and work – they deserve respect. Trust has to be earned and reciprocated. Participants may come from different backgrounds, have very different occupations, even different political leanings, but the process is designed to ensure that single-issue preoccupations take second place to a broad-based vision that is the result of genuine collaboration. Similarly, participants must respect other groups' and individuals' views and their right to express them as a starting point for working towards a shared vision.

The professional team members must value community input, whether they agree with it or not. Ideas should be tested, not summarily rejected. Explanations should be provided when suggestions cannot be incorporated in the plans.

At Kew Bridge, a well-organised and previously opposed local community became engaged in a charrette process and design development forums. This led to a redesigned scheme and the delivery of a new gateway development on a site that had been vacant for a long time.

Some development proposals are opposed by communities who begrudge the change to their neighbourhood, over which they feel they have little or no control. This can stoke up negativity and antagonism, sometimes resulting in campaigns and even public demonstrations. An open and transparent charrette process will not automatically dispel the hostility, but it can be effective in bringing people together to build positive consensus visions and action plans, taking account of diverse views.

13
DRAWING, ILLUSTRATION AND MODELS

A charrette differs from traditional consultation meetings and exhibitions because the process includes the physical activity of drawing, in addition to the written and oral activity of discussion workshops.

Although the co-design planning sessions can encourage members of the public to put pen to paper, it is the skill of the facilitator that most often helps tease out and sketch ideas from participants. A suggestion may or may not work when it is drawn on to a plan, but the fact that it has been sketched enables the community to see their ideas immediately and understand the implications of certain decisions. Colour is important, and the simple illustration of water features and areas of green space can help bring a two-dimensional design alive, even to lay-people who may have no experience of urban design.

Once masterplan designs have been worked up in more detail, it can be very useful to build a three-dimensional scale model of the proposed development. This can help people understand the concept of height and mass and show the potential impact of new buildings on surrounding neighbourhoods. In The Liberties in Dublin a model was built of the area following the charrette process and was very effective in helping participants appreciate the scale of development proposals in context.

14
SITE VISITS AND WALKABOUTS

A charrette is an action-oriented process, not an academic exercise. It should, where possible, include the potential to visit the site, so that participants can see the site through the 'lens of placemaking', and observe closely the constraints and opportunities of a specific place. Members of the professional team should be on hand to explain key issues, and participants can gain valuable insight into the site's context, such as key views and connections. At Caddington in Bedfordshire, the site visits were key for participants to appreciate the character and screened nature of the site.

This practical observation is useful when the team returns to the charrette venue to draw up design options for the site. Adjacent buildings that may be retained are remembered as elements of 'setting', and roads which are usually driven down in a journey from A to B take on a totally different significance when viewed in terms of access to a site.

15
FOLLOW-UP

The collaborative and stimulating nature of a charrette creates a sense of momentum and raises expectations, which need to be managed positively. Some process 'follow-up' should be planned and resourced before the charrette takes place, so that members of the community, who have often invested considerable personal time and effort in the process, do not feel let down.

Public sector planning and regeneration projects in particular can take a long time to deliver results, and communities will need patience. But if time passes and nothing happens, patience may be replaced by anger and frustration.

'Early win' and 'meanwhile' or 'interim' projects, sometimes known as pop-up or tactical urbanism, are useful ways to keep projects alive and build confidence that the process can deliver results. The fact that the local vet could move temporarily into a barrack block while the Caterham Village was being developed was a visible reminder of the original charrette.

In Scarborough a Town Team was set up whose first task was the development of a charter to embed the principles of the charrette into a document signed up to by the town.

Involvement in creating design codes, for example, can help remind people that they still have a role to play in the development process, however distant the delivery.

16
VALUABLE MEMORIES

Communities that have been through a charrette process often retain a strong memory of the experience as a special time when people came together in the spirit of collaboration at the birth of the project. The vision becomes a tangible expression of the process itself.

The fact that it is an intensive event adds to the uniqueness of the memory. People who were strangers at the first workshop can become firm friends by the time of the report back, a week or so later. Knowledge is acquired, unexpected skills are developed, and community champions emerge to help take the project forward.

At Midland, Perth the original vision is regularly referred to some twenty years later, and held firmly in mind by both the community and the Redevelopment Authority.

17
NOT REVERTING TO TOP-DOWN APPROACHES, REMAINING PARTICIPATIVE

There is always a danger that a development team may choose to revert to a traditional closed planning process, even after a charrette has been successfully held earlier in a process. This could be due to various factors, including staff changes, or because it is considered that a charrette approach would take too long. A community will resent the change of style if they have already experienced an open, collaborative way of working. This can lead to conflict and delay, and it is undoubtedly a short-sighted approach.

At Alder Hey a later stage of the planning of the scheme's residential areas was developed without a charrette and resulted in opposition to a scheme from a community that had been very supportive of the earlier phases, and were indeed actively and positively involved in delivering the new park as part of the scheme.

18

PROJECT DELIVERY AND GOVERNANCE

A natural follow-on from community participation in charrette processes is the involvement of local communities in the further development of proposals and the eventual delivery, ownership and management of sustainable and locally responsive community assets. A revised version of Sherry Arnstein's ladder of participation by John Thompson illustrates the successive stages that people can move through to reach the point where they feel truly identified with and in control of neighbourhood decision making.

Organisations are being established globally following charrettes to enable the continuing involvement of the community in project design, budgeting, delivery and management. Structures include Community Forums, Town Teams, Community Trusts Community Land Trusts and parish and town councils. Community Land Trusts are becoming increasingly important methods of delivering affordable enterprise space, community facilities and housing. At Caddington Woods, for example, a new Community Trust will own and manage over forty homes, a community building and the open spaces and woodland as well as providing a new bus service linking to the local town and villages.

19

SPREADING THE WORD

Charrettes remain a surprisingly non-mainstream way of working, despite their emergence fifty years ago as a proven and valuable aid to planning and design. Perhaps this is because they have never received the mainstream political and media attention they deserve. Maybe there are not enough skilled professionals to facilitate processes. Or perhaps planners are threatened by a process that challenges the status quo.

Charrettes encourage dialogue, clarity and transparency of purpose. Those who have organised them, or who have experienced their benefits, need to be encouraged to promote them – by speaking at conferences, submitting award nominations, writing articles and books, and lobbying politicians.

The rise of social media and blogging could be a way for stories of successful charrettes to reach a new audience. The aim must be to spread the word to the wider community, to awaken debate, to generate commissions and to inspire confidence in the value of a collaborative and participatory planning process.

20

CHANGING LIVES AND CAREERS

The case studies involved a number of participants who readily acknowledged the impact the process had on shaping their lives and future careers, from a professional perspective or through community activism and taking on responsible roles.

In Nashville and Santa Fe the architects are still very much involved in the long-running regeneration processes, and in the minds of the community are linked with the project.

At Caddington a former community activist, now councillor, has a role on the Community Trust established to deliver affordable housing, environmental management and a new bus service from the site.

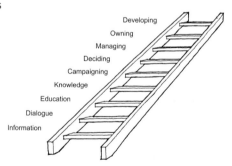

FIGURE 6.1:
Ladder of participation

ENDNOTES

1   Bill Caudill, interviewed by Larry Meyer for an Oral Business History Project, University of Texas, 1971. Sponsored by The Moody Foundation. Source: CRS Archives, CRS Center, Texas A&M University, College Station, TX

2   President John F. Kennedy, inaugural address, Washington DC, 20 January 1961

3   Joel Mills, American Institute of Architects, 2017

4   Jane Jacobs, *The Death and Life of Great American Cities*, New York: Vintage Books, 1992, page 238

5   Nate Berg, 'David Lewis: Urban Design Pioneer', Citylab.com, 25 January 2012

6   Peter Batchelor and David Lewis, 'Urban Design in Action', North Carolina State University, 1986, page 4

7   Sherry R. Arnstein, 'A Ladder of Citizen Participation', *Journal of the American Institute of Planners*, vol. 35, no. 4, July 1969, pages 216–224

8   Interview with Ray Gindroz, February 2012, Alexandria, VA.

9   Nabeel Hamdi, *The Placemaker's Guide to Building Community*, London: Earthscan, 2010, page 223

10 Remaking Cities: Proceedings of the 1988 International Conference in Pittsburgh, University of Pittsburgh Press, 1989, page 1

11 Congress for New Urbanism, https://www.cnu.org/who-we-are/charter-new-urbanism, 'The Charter of the New Urbanism', 2013

12 Interview with David Lewis, 21 April 2015, Pittsburgh, PA

13 G. Brown and R. Gifford, 'Architects predict lay evaluations of large contemporary buildings: whose conceptual properties?', *Journal of Environmental Psychology,* no. 21, 2001, pages 93–99; J. Darke, 'Architects and user requirements in public-sector housing: 3 Towards an adequate understanding of user requirements in housing' *Environment and Planning B: Planning and Design*, no. 11, 1984 pages 389–433

14 David Halpern, *Mental Health and the Built Environment: More than Bricks and Mortar?* New York: Routledge, 2013

15 Charles Montgomery, *Happy City: Transforming Our Lives Through Urban Design,* London: Penguin, 2013

16 'Housing Communities: What People Want', Prince's Foundation, London, 2014, page 15

17 National Charrette Institute, charretteinstitute.org/nci-april-news, 'The Zen of Charrettes', 22 April 2016

18 International Association for Public Participation, http://www.iap2.org/?page=corevalues, 'Core Values for the Practice of Public Participation'

19 *John O'Groat Journal*, Friday 1 March 2013

IMAGE CREDITS

TITLE PAGE
Top left JTP; top right AIA;
centre left DPZ; centre right JTP;
bottom left Miller Research; bottom right JTP

PREFACE
p.xii Left JTP; Top right GILLESPIES; Centre JTP; Bottom right
    Urbanismplus;
p.xiii Charles Campion JTP

CHAPTER 3
p.14 JTP

CHAPTER 4
p.18 National Charrette Institute;
p.22 JTP;
pp.25-29 JTP

CHAPTER 5
p.38 Jesse Nusbaum. Soldiers at railroad depot, General Bell's visit
    regarding "Taos Rebellion, Santa Fe, New Mexico", 1913. Courtesy of
    the Palace of the Governors Photo Archives (NMHM/DCA), 061433;
p.40 AIA;
p.41 JTP;
p.42 Victor Patterson;
p.43 JTP;
p.48 Western Australian Government;
p.49 Ecologically Sustainable Design Pty. Ltd;
p.51 Western Australian Government;
p.52 Bristol Branch of the Grenadier Guards Association;
pp.53-55 JTP;
p.56 Released into the public domain by Ryan Kaldari;
pp.57-58 AIA;
p.59 JTP;
p.60 JTP;
PP.62-65 JTP;
pp.66-67 Alta Consulting;
p.68 JTP;
p.69 Alta Consulting;
p.70 City of Vancouver Archives, donated by Donn B.A. Williams in 1987;
p.71 Wesgroup;
pp.71-72 DPZ;

p.72 Wesgroup;
p.73 JTP;
p.74 Alder Hey Hospital;
pp.75-76 A Princes Foundation for Building Community;
p.76 Eleanor Brogan;
p.77 JTP;
pp.78-80 JTP;
p.81 Craig Auckland / Fotohaus;
p.82 Released into the public domain by Innomann;
p.83 Arie Overes;
p.84 JTP;
p.85 Debbie Radcliffe;
p.86 Guinness Archive, Diageo Ireland;
pp.87-89 JTP;
pp.90-93 Miller Research;
pp.92-93 Howard Bowcott;
p.94 Alexander Turnbull Library, Wellington, New Zealand;
pp.95-96 Urbanismplus;
p.96 Gerrard O'Brien;
p.97 Planning Quarterly, photo by Richard White;
p.98 DSRL and the NDA;
p.99 The Keasbury-Gordon Photograph Archive;
p.99 JTP/ Gillespies;
pp.99-100 JTP;
p.102 Courtesy of Dumfries Museum;
p.102 CP17/063 British Geological Survey © NERC 2017. All rights
    reserved;
pp.103-105 Gillespies LLP;
pp.106-107 Courtesy of Vauxhall Heritage;
pp.108-109 JTP;
p.109 David Kennedy, Place Images;
p.110 Andrew Wilson;
pp.111-112 JTP;
p.113 Barnes Town Team;
p.113 One-World Design Architects;
p.114 Shujie Chen, JTP;
pp.115-117 JTP;
pp.118-121 JTP

CHAPTER 6
p.130 JTP

INDEX